PLAYING WITH NO REGRETS: MENTAL SECRETS FOR UNLOCKING YOUR TENNIS POTENTIAL

This book is for tennis players who want to break through the mental barriers holding them back

by David Zobler and Tom Aguilar

Copyright © 2024 David Zobler and Tom Aguilar
All rights reserved.

Acknowledgements

Cover photos (from left to right) Jonathan Fromkin, Michelle Eisenberg, and Jake Ly.

The authors would like to thank both the players and coaches for taking the time to help complete this book and provide their insights and wisdom regarding the mental side of tennis.

Dedication

I dedicate this book to my parents, Ludwik and Phyllis Zobler, who introduced me to the sport, were my number one fans, and motivated me to continue to love the game.
David

I dedicate this book to my dad, Arnold Aguilar, for patiently learning and teaching me the game, and to my mom, Noelle Aguilar, for supporting me from afar with love and prayers (she couldn't watch me play a match, it made her too nervous). I miss you both every day.
Tom

Contents

Acknowledgements iii
Dedication iv
Contents v
Foreword xi
Preface xv
Understand why you lose 1
Top 20 reasons you lose 3
   #1: Not believing you have what it takes to win 3
   #2: Unwilling to change a losing game plan 6
   #3: Paralysis by over-analysis 8
   #4: Placing too much importance on outcomes (a.k.a.: winning) 9
   #5: Tensing up or "choking" 12
   #6: Not respecting your opponent's game (a.k.a.; taking your opponent too lightly) 14
   #7: Destructive self-talk 16
   #8: Not able to move on (after losing a big game, getting a bad call, etc.) 17
   #9: Losing focus 19
   #10: Playing the excuse game 20
   #11: Playing not to lose 22
   #12: Dwelling on your losses (instead of learning from them) 24
   #13: Viewing competition as a threat, not a challenge . 27
   #14: Not following a mental and physical pre-match routine 29

#15: Your game and conditioning need work 32

#16: You don't make your opponent earn the big points 35

#17: Throwing in the towel when you're not playing your best 37

#18: Failing to maintain a positive mind and body language between points and games 39

#19: Lack of consistency 42

#20: Lack of a game plan (not playing to your strengths and your opponent's weaknesses) 43

Key character traits to becoming a winner on and off the court 69

What does "winning" mean in the landscape of highly competitive junior tennis and beyond? 74

Moving from destructive to productive self-talk 83

Managing your emotions 87

What does it mean to be mentally tough? 90

Mentally tough athletes… 94

Mindfulness and peak athletic performance 106

Using proper breathing, visualizations and rituals to gain a competitive edge 115

    Proper breathing 115

    Visualization 116

    Rituals 120

Does your confidence and self-belief hold you back from reaching your potential? 123

Would you be crazy to see a sports psychologist? 129

Experts' bios 137
    Peter Smith's bio: 137
    Jeff Salzenstein's bio: 137
    Mark Merklein's bio: 138
    Diego Ayala's bio: 139
    George Bezecny's bio: 140
    Jack Bauerle's bio: 140
    Brett Kurtz's bio: 141
    Alexandra Osborne's bio 141
    Jeff Thomsen's bio 142
    Steve Adamson's bio 142
    Larry Willens' bio 143

Experts' winning tips for players 144
    Peter Smith's winning tips for players 145
    Jeff Salzenstein's winning tips for players 146
    Mark Merklein's winning tips for players 148
    Diego Ayala's winning tips for players 150
    George Bezecny's winning tips for players 151
    Bruce Kurtz's winning tips for players 152
    Alexandra Osborne's winning tips for players 153
    Jeff Thomsen's winning tips for players 154
    Steve Adamson's winning tips for players 155
    Larry Willens' winning tips for players 155

Experts' winning tips for coaches 157
    Peter Smith's winning tips for coaches 157

Jeff Salzenstein's winning tips for coaches 160

Mark Merklein's winning tips for coaches 161

Diego Ayala's winning tips for coaches 162

Jack Bauerle's winning tips for coaches 163

Brett Kurtz's winning tips for coaches.......................165

Jeff Thomsen's winning tips for coaches...................166

Steve Adamson's winning tips for coaches 167

Larry Willens' winning tips for coaches....................167

Player and coach interview highlights............................169

Player interview highlights...169

Coach interview highlights 183

Parting shots: key takeaways, common themes, and surprises 187

#1 - Mental skills/mental toughness training doesn't get the attention it deserves..............................187

#2 – Seeking instant gratification is your enemy 188

#3 – Training your mind to focus on the present will lead to improved results and more fun competing 189

#4 – Being able to refocus quickly is critical to your success 190

#5 - Effective breathing is an underrated asset 191

#6 - Players benefit from taking ownership for their tennis results and developing their game 191

#7 - Elite tennis players struggle with issues of self-confidence, self-doubt, nerves and anxiousness just like the rest of us do. 193

#8 - Perfectionism is a common problem for high achieving tennis players 194

#9 - Play to win, not to avoid losing! 196

About the authors 198

    David Zobler 199

    Tom Aguilar 200

Index 202

(This page intentionally left blank.)

Foreword

For those who don't know me, my name is Peter Smith. I have been fortunate enough to stay in the game of tennis my whole adult life. I have had the privilege of coaching hundreds of young men at four incredible universities: Long Beach State, Fresno State, Pepperdine, and USC. I always tried to learn from our wins and losses. I am still learning, still trying to get better.

I have coached players on the grandest stage in the game against the greatest players of all time (Steve Johnson vs Federer — Wimbledon, 2016 round of 16). I have also coached thousands of juniors (boys and girls) privately and publicly. Tennis is tennis whether it is played at a Grand Slam or a local park. An incredible match between two minds – a physical version of chess.

The most challenging part of tennis is controlling your mind and your emotions. There is a saying that tennis is all about the head and the feet. To players just starting it seems impossible because all the strokes are so challenging. You can master those but what you will always be working on is your positioning and controlling your thoughts. Even the best players have their tough days with these issues. Remember that you, like your tennis, are always a work in progress. You will never be perfect and that is the journey you should enjoy about tennis – that challenge. Tennis is an imperfect game played by imperfect people. There will never be a perfect tennis match – remember that and enjoy the journey.

David and Tom did an outstanding job in this book spelling out why the mental game is every bit as important as the physical game. I fully endorse the strategies presented for developing a mentally tough mindset. Their ideas on mindfulness, self-talk and how and why to stay in the present were particularly powerful.

The top twenty reasons for losing were also dead on. It captured the key reasons why players lose matches, underperform and don't reach their potential. Reading and applying the concepts in this book will help players and coaches turn the tables and win more matches.

I also loved what they had to say about competing, enjoying the process, and never getting caught up in what others may think about your performance. This is critical to winning in tennis and in life.

At times, I have failed heroically at the mental game, but I always got up the next day and tried as hard or harder than I did the day before. I have been in many situations where I really felt like it was life or death. I know it wasn't but that is how it literally felt. Finals of National Collegiate Athlete Association (NCAAs) or Finals of National Father-Son tournaments. You want to feel pressure? Go hold serve with your kid at net with a Gold Ball on the line.

The truth of it is pressure is how you view the situation. When you win and have your dreams come true you realize it's nice but there are victories in losing and the real victory is being in the arena and taking part in the contest. In those moments I always knew I was the luckiest guy in the world, doing something I loved with people I loved. Now that is the ultimate victory.

Read and learn the lessons compiled in this book and I believe you will enjoy the ride as much as I have.

Peter Smith, coach of 5 NCAA championship teams

- Coach of Steve Johnson – GOAT of College Tennis

- Coach of Robert Farah – World #1 doubles player – first player ever to win a Grand Slam for Columbia winning 2019 Wimbledon and US Open

- Coach of countless other great players who you will never hear of, but I am so proud of them for overcoming obstacles and becoming great versions of themselves on and off the court.

- Coach of my 3 children; Tanner, Riley, and Colter who all love the game and who all carried me to a National Championship in Father-Son tennis.

Peter Smith with sons Tanner and Riley.

(This page intentionally left blank.)

Preface

Background on why I wrote this book—David Zobler

"It's one-on-one out there man. There ain't no hiding. I can't pass the ball."—Pete Sampras

My athletic career started off quite well. When I was 8 to 9 years old, I was the star of my town's football team, winning the most valuable player (MVP) two years in a row. I was a running back, and few kids could match my speed, quickness, strength, and sure hands. I also excelled in other organized youth sports in my pre-teen years including baseball, lacrosse, and soccer. I had no shortage of confidence in my athletic ability and had high expectations as well as big dreams for what I could achieve athletically.

When I reached my teen years, I went through puberty late, and the athletic advantages I once had seemed to be disappearing. Yes, I was still very fast, but my peers all seemed to be growing faster than I was. Also, my dad made it clear he didn't want me to play high school football – like many parents, he was afraid I would hurt myself.

My dad, being an avid tennis player and fan, encouraged me to pursue tennis. He took me to the US Open every year and I was a big fan of players like Jimmy Connors, John McEnroe, and Bjorn Borg. I had some talent at tennis and excelled against most of the kids in my home town in Long Island, New York. By age 14, I had quit football and decided to focus primarily on tennis.

I have vivid memories of playing local USTA tennis tournaments as a teenager. Although I played well in practice, I was not able to consistently translate that into match play. I also suffered from a lack of self-confidence, partially attributable to going through puberty late. In addition, I was very shy around girls as a teenager.

In tournament play, I suffered through a repeated pattern of getting so tense and nervous that I would invariably double fault on important points and/or my body would become so stiff I couldn't swing my racquet naturally. I would try to convince myself before matches to just go out there and have fun, but once I got out on the court, I would inevitably want to win so badly that my nerves would kick in and I couldn't play up to my capability. I felt somewhat helpless in overcoming my propensity to underperform and didn't have a coach or sports psychologist to lean on to get over the mental hurdles I faced.

One of the reasons I wanted to win so badly was to make my parents proud. This put added pressure on myself, especially when they were watching my matches. My nerves didn't seem to get in the way much when I participated in other sports, however, including high school soccer and track and field. At the time, I couldn't quite understand what made tennis unique, other than the fact I was out there on my own.

As a high school senior, I thought I had finally overcome my tendencies to self-destruct on the court for good. I worked hard and gained more confidence in my serve and led my high school team to its first undefeated season in school history. I capped off the year by winning the decisive match in the conference championship, winning the 3rd set 6-0. My confidence had grown as I ended my high school career.

I was able to make my college tennis team as a walk-on (I played for a division 3 powerhouse at the time, SUNY at

Albany), and earned a starting position at 6th singles my freshman year. By my senior year I was playing 2nd singles, but I never felt I fully lived up to my potential during my college playing career.

Although I had some good moments as a college tennis player my bout with nerves (and muscle cramps) started to rear its ugly head again. One college match was particularly mentally scarring – I was ahead 5-0 in the first set against a rival school (Binghamton University) and then the wheels completely fell off. I got more and more tight as the match went on and lost 7-5 and 6-2. I also painfully recall another tough match against Army that if I had won, the team would have secured the victory. I felt awful as I believed I had let my teammates down.

Interestingly, just about everyone I interviewed in writing this book felt they hadn't lived up to their potential or personal expectations for one reason or another. Do we all think we are better or more talented than we really are? Is the sport so mentally and emotionally tough that it's simply very challenging to realize our aspirations? What holds us back? Does it come down to self-confidence, discipline, perseverance, physical gifts, coaching or some combination of those factors? Part of my motivation for writing this book was to find answers to these questions.

Although I never lost my love for the game of tennis, I did struggle mightily at times losing matches I felt I had no business losing during my junior days and college tennis career. Over time, I dramatically improved my mental game and was able to overcome what had often plagued me in my younger playing days. With my improved mental skills and confidence in my late 20s and beyond, I achieved my best tennis results.

I taught myself how to breathe properly, practiced using rituals during matches and became much better at not get sucked into negative thought patterns that would sometimes bring me down. Essentially, I had turned a weakness into a competitive advantage, as now I would estimate I win 75% of close matches because of my mental toughness.

I'd like to pass along what I have learned and observed from playing and studying the game and coaching others in this book. I also want to continue to learn from others how to become even more mentally tough and play smarter.

My passion for the game increased as I improved my mental toughness skills, and I learned to love to compete and push myself more than ever to achieve personal excellence. I'd like to see highly competitive players benefit from my personal experience and others' experiences to maximize their results and have more fun and joy while doing so.

In this book, I'll share some of my personal insights, and more importantly, share lessons from outstanding coaches and players. In particular, a large portion of this book focuses on why we lose on the tennis court (note: a lot of this carries over off the court too) and what we can learn from experts to achieve greater success and personal satisfaction.

Understand why you lose

"Once you find that peace, that place of peace and quiet, harmony and confidence, that's when you start playing your best."—Roger Federer

"The important thing is to learn a lesson every time you lose. Life is a learning process, and you have to try to learn what's best for you. Let me tell you, life is not fun when you're banging your head against a brick wall all the time."—John McEnroe

Do you lose matches you think you should win? Have you "choked" or gotten the "yips" on more than one occasion? Are you unable to play your best tennis when the stakes are the highest? If you answered yes to any of these questions you are not alone.

Let's face it. To be successful, grow and thrive as a competitive tennis player, you are going to have to endure your share of defeats. The smart tennis player, however, reflects after each loss on what he could have done differently to achieve a better result next time out. Of course, in some cases, the answer is nothing. Sometimes, you run up against a superior opponent, or perhaps someone who is playing lights out on that day. That's not what this book is about though. This book will help you understand why you lose (or self-destruct), and what is in your power to do before, during and after each match to play your best tennis when the pressure is more consistently on.

So, why do we lose matches that we *should or could* win? Based on my research as well as personal experience participating, observing, and coaching competitive tennis, there are twenty important reasons for losing, under-performing and not playing to your potential.

We'll cover these common reasons for losing or underperforming (among others) on the pages ahead and provide key tips on what you can do behaviorally, tactically, and strategically to avoid these pitfalls, enjoy competing more, and ultimately, improve your game and win more matches. Let's get to it!

Top 20 reasons you lose

#1: Not believing you have what it takes to win

"Tennis is mostly mental. You win or lose the match before you even go out there."—Venus Williams

"Tennis is a mental game. Everyone is fit, everyone hits great forehands and backhands."—Novak Djokovic

"Tennis is 90% mental."—Jimmy Connors

If you find yourself ahead in a match and lack confidence, you may start thinking to yourself, "Am I really capable of beating this guy"? He is ranked higher than I am and is a better player." A thought pattern like this can begin to manifest itself in the warm up by becoming overly impressed with your opponent's game, or even before you step foot on the court if perhaps you've gone online and checked out his or her previous results or ranking.

Successful tennis players believe they can win and are fully capable and deserving of winning. This belief is a fundamental, critical ingredient for competitive success. In essence, this is all about self-confidence. As Sloane Stephens, former US Open Champion, commented: *"When you have confidence, you can do anything."*

But, what can you do to boost your self-confidence as a tennis player? The best way is probably getting over the hump by coming through in an important match. A good example of this on the professional level was when former great, Ivan Lendl, finally broke through to win his first Grand Slam title after losing his previous four Grand Slam finals. Lendl then went on to win 7 more majors. Winning leads to more winning and higher personal expectations and can be habit forming. Conversely, losing has the potential to lower one's expectations and/or leads to more negative thought patterns and continued losing.

Paul Goldstein, former ATP pro and current Stanford University men's coach, noted: *"When I was winning a lot, I had more confidence. Winning begets more confidence. I didn't think as much, and I trusted myself more.* ***Winning was the best medicine or panacea for having a state of calm come over my body"***. (Source: Weechats.com, August 14, 2015).

Positive self-talk both before and during your matches can also help raise your confidence which we will cover in this book. If you find yourself ahead or close to potentially winning against a supposedly "superior" player, you are certainly more than capable of pulling off the upset. Your self-talk could be something like: "I've trained hard and I can do this. I'm going to win this match. I just need to keep doing what I am doing." Sports psychologists and coaches can also be very helpful in improving your self-talk and self-confidence on and off the court. We'll get into this more later in the book.

George Mumford, author of "The Mindful Athlete: Secrets to Pure Performance" noted**:** *"I'm constantly amazed at the number of athletes I work with who are exceptionally skilled and highly talented, but don't play that way because they don't see themselves that way. They don't have a clear sense of purpose or understand how they see themselves creates their reality. If you tell yourself that you are not good compared to others, your self-concept probably needs re-examining."*

Dr. Allen Fox, author "Tennis: Winning the Mental Match", does not believe it is necessary that you expect to win every time you go out as that may be unrealistic. However, he says that it is necessary that you at least believe "there is hope" that you can win.

Great champions like Roger Federer, Rafael Nadal, and Novak Djokovic always maintain the belief and confidence they can win despite difficult odds. These three great champions have won an extraordinary number of matches when only a point or two away from defeat.

For the rest of us, it is not uncommon to have some doubt in the front or the back of our mind that you really have what it takes to win or are even deserving of winning. Even professionals and other highly accomplished players have these doubts creep in from time to time based on my research and interviews in writing this book.

Darrin Donnelly, author of "Victory Favors the Fearless", points out: *"You've got to counter the voice of fear with the voice of faith. Fear tells you that you don't have the talent or whatever else you think you need to be successful. Fear says you are not good enough; you don't deserve success. It also tells you to not aim too high."* Donnelly suggests you fight fear by telling yourself you have everything you need to be successful, and that you have the power to make or break your future.

To be clear, you can still achieve success when you don't win. If you truly believe in yourself and aim as high as possible, you give yourself a chance to reach your full potential. In other words, success is being the very best you can be. Donnelly noted: *"I can't guarantee that self-confidence will ensure you victory, but I can guarantee that self-doubt will ensure you defeat."*

#2: Unwilling to change a losing game plan

"You need to be quick on making the right decisions, analyze what's happening."—Rafael Nadal

Be honest. Are you open and always willing to change your strategy and tactics during matches? A common example I see is players who like to hit big shots and play aggressively, and this game plan or approach generally works well. But not today! Maybe it's because you are a little off your game, or perhaps your opponent thrives on the pace you are generating. A situation like this, calls for a willingness to be more flexible. Some players, however, are simply unwilling or unable to show the patience or flexibility needed to rethink their tactics. The successful player will consider what strategies can be deployed to improve his/her play and/or bring down the opponent's game, rather than sticking with a losing formula and hoping things will somehow turn themselves around. Hope is not a recipe for success!

A change in tactics may be just the trick needed to bring down your opponent's play and confidence. I vividly recall playing a challenge match in college and noticed my opponent's overhead was shaky and inconsistent. I also noticed he became visibly frustrated whenever he missed an overhead. When the match got tight, I brought him into the net and repeatedly lobbed him. After he missed a few overheads, the rest of his game quickly went downhill, and I turned a close match into an easy win. The point being, winning is not simply based on how well you play. If you can figure out tactics to bring your opponent's game down a notch or two it will greatly enhance your chances of winning. On the other hand, if you are losing and keep doing the same things and are unwilling to change a losing game plan, nine out of ten times you will lose.

Winning players are comfortable or at least willing to problem solve during the match by paying attention to what is working and what is not. Think of it as a puzzle to be solved and have an open mind that there is always a solution. Sometimes it's as simple as keeping the ball deep and down the middle. Other times, if you have an opponent who is more comfortable camping out on the baseline, you'll want to occasionally hit short slices or drop shots to force your opponent out of his/her comfort zone and make him/her come into the net. The point is, by paying attention to what is working (and not working!), you can take that intelligence and exploit it throughout the match.

Of course, to be able to change a losing game plan, it's helpful to have a well-rounded game and a variety of weapons at your disposal. It's not enough though to have weapons you are only comfortable deploying when you are ahead. You need to have the confidence to use all your weapons whether you are up 4 games to 1 in the first set or tied at 4-4 in the third set.

If you have a Plan B, C, and D on the tennis court, the failure of Plan A is unlikely to cause despair. Tennis players often lose because at least a part of them secretly (or not so secretly) gives up. You are less likely to psychologically give up if you have something else in your bag of tricks to try. Practice playing every part of the court and hitting every kind of shot with a variety of spins. You'll likely uncover a weakness you can exploit if you have all these shots in your arsenal.

#3: Paralysis by over-analysis

"I stopped thinking too much about what could happen and relied on my physical and mental strength to play the right shots at the right time."—Novak Djokovic

When playing tennis, it's good to think tactically and strategically during your matches. It's not helpful, however, to be thinking (or obsessing!) about your stroke mechanics in competitive situations (note: it is okay during practice sessions though). Focusing on stroke mechanics will most certainly cause more muscle tension and result in poorer performance. Generally, what we think about is what we worry about!

As Dr. Michelle Cleere, clinical psychologist, points out: *"You cannot think and perform (at your peak) at the same time. Thinking pulls you right out of whatever you are doing. It increases your heart rate. An increase in heart rate leads to hard, shallow breathing which leads to a lack of oxygen. Thinking tightens and tenses your muscles. Your range of motion narrows. Thinking also decreases focus."*

Therefore, once you step foot on the court to play a match, it's best to keep things as simple as possible and not clutter your mind with too many details. If you are trying to incorporate new techniques (such as a change in your service motion or grip) it can be more challenging to keep your mind and self-instruction completely quiet.

If you find yourself having difficulty keeping your mind off stoke mechanics, try to focus on other things such as watching the ball or what you want to do tactically (make your opponent hit high backhands, hit a high percentage of first serves, etc.). Too many complicated self-instructions or over-analysis will inevitably increase your muscle tension and lead to poorer play.

Remember this phrase: "Simplicity leads to consistency". Simplicity in your stroke mechanics also means your strokes are less likely to break down under pressure.

Similarly, simplicity in your thought processes means less tension and overthinking when you are in a pressure filled situation. As Peter Smith, former USC coach, pointed out when I interviewed him, sometimes players get in their own way by overthinking things. The coach may be able to help the player remove any mental interference getting in the way. He commented: *"You are out there on your own and trying to figure things out can be tricky. It's better to keep the game plan very simple so the player will be comfortable with it."*

#4: Placing too much importance on outcomes (a.k.a.: winning)

"You can't be afraid to miss, and you can't be afraid to lose, otherwise, you're never going to be able to play your best tennis."— Rafael Nadal

"Freed from the thoughts of winning, I instantly play better. I stop thinking, start feeling. My shots become a half-second quicker, my decisions become the product of instinct rather than logic."—Andre Agassi

"Being afraid to lose is about your ego."—Paul Annacone

"When you want things so badly, sometimes you can't handle the pressure." – Maria Sakkari**,** WTA top 10 player

It is a good thing to want to win, but it can work against you if you place too much importance on it. **Wanting to win too much is akin to being afraid to lose.** It also is unhealthy if your self-esteem is directly tied to your tennis results! As Jim Courier, former tennis great and commentator, pointed out, *"It's very, very dangerous to have your self-worth riding on your results as an athlete."* Ironically, you will perform better if you are less concerned with the results (winning) and more focused on the process (focusing on what you want to do tactically, competing, etc.). The mere thought process of thinking about winning or losing the match means your mind is not focused on the present (e.g., next point).

Placing too much emphasis on winning can easily lead to an emotional roller coaster of ups and downs and gets in the way of enjoying the game and the competition. Sometimes you may feel pressure because you don't want to let other people down, rather than concern over letting yourself down. If you are on a tennis team, you naturally don't want to let your teammates down by losing. For children and teens, a common pattern I've also seen is a fear of letting your parents or coaches down. After all, they may have invested a lot of time and money in your tennis game. If you are a parent or coach of a junior tournament player, remember to not place emphasis on the wins and losses.

Paul Annacone, coach of Pete Sampras, Roger Federer and Taylor Fritz, commented in the Netflix Series "Break Point": *"The methodology has to be that you don't want it too bad, because self-imposed pressure is the biggest catalyst to paralyze your ability to maximize your talent."*

Former ATP pro and tennis coach, Diego Ayala, noted that even pros in their mid to late 20s can be too caught up in what parents or agents want, and this just adds to the pressure to win. He commented: *"The pressure (from parents and agents) leads to crapping out on the courts."*

Any time you are trying too hard it results in more stress, tension and stiffness, and it makes it impossible to play smoothly and effortlessly. It also depletes your energy. I believe one of the most common reasons for feeling you need to win is to save your ego because you are worried about what others will think of you if you lose. Because of that worry, you may play it safe or play small, rather than playing your game the way you are capable of. Intellectually, you know it's only a tennis match, but it feels much more than that when your heart is pounding, your breathing rate has changed, and you are sweating like you are being chased in a dark alley.

When I see a player who is too caught up with winning (or fear of losing), I might ask him "what's the worst thing that could happen if you lose" or "why is it so important that you win"? If you can get the player to talk it through, it can help put things into perspective, reduce stress over potentially losing, and put him in a better position to play up to his capability. On a related note, when coaching players, it's important that they want to win for the right reasons (i.e., they are passionate about the game and improving, they love to compete, etc.), rather than the wrong reasons (i.e., not wanting to disappoint their parents or to live up to someone else's lofty expectations).

In an ideal world, tennis players would have a "process" instead of an "outcome" attitude, meaning they would only focus on what they need to do to perform their best. A process attitude focuses on what is controllable during match play, and reduces doubt, worry, and anxiety.

The problem is that results do matter, and we are in a competitive sport that resides in a competitive culture. It is not realistic for competitive tennis players to be completely process-focused.

In addition, *"athletes who think failure is not an option will eventually experience some form of emotional burnout or put incredible levels of pressure on themselves by creating an unattainable standard of perfection and are emotionally exhausted all the time because nothing they do is ever good enough."* (Source: Medicalxpress.com). Coaches and parents can be helpful by reinforcing effort and personal development as opposed to meeting the personal standards of someone else. As for the athletes, **remember to be kind to yourself and accept that mistakes and adversity are a natural part of the performance process** (Source: John Dunn, University of Alberta). You have only failed if you have failed to learn, and facing adversity is a great way to learn and reach a higher level of motivation.

I believe Peter Smith captured the optimal mindset when he commented: *"I like to compete more than I like to win. True competitors want to compete more than win."* **If tennis players can remain focused on competing rather than on winning, they will invariably enjoy the battle more, and feel less stress to win.**

#5: Tensing up or "choking"

"The only pressure I feel is what I put on myself."—Andy Roddick

"Choking is being in a position to win, and then experiencing some critical failure of nerve or spirit. That

never happened to me. And I can't help but think it was because I was never afraid to lose."—Pete Sampras

In my experience, tensing up or choking is often a byproduct of other factors (e.g., being afraid to lose, not being able to quiet your brain, etc.). In general, we play our best tennis when we are relaxed, focused and fully immersed in what we are doing (this is well documented in W. Timothy Gallwey's book, "The Inner Game of Tennis"). Bill Cole, author of "The Mental Game of Tennis" also pointed out, "*You are in the zone when you have a calm mental state, pure focus, relaxation, your mind is in the here and now and you are allowing your performance to happen*." In other words, **let your muscle memory take over and avoid overthinking things**.

The truth is you can't completely avoid tensing up or choking. Even the top pros get tight on occasion when things aren't going their way. As Jim Courier remarked on TV, *"it doesn't matter how many times you succeed, you still feel the pressure."* Even the great Roger Federer got tight in a Wimbledon final against Novak Djokovic when he had two match points.

If you feel yourself getting overly nervous or tense, your footwork will also typically suffer. Conversely, if you can get your feet moving, this can be a good way to alleviate some of your nervousness.

Former top 100 pro, Jeff Salzenstein, believes one key to managing your body's tension is to maintain awareness of your hand tension. He noted: *"Most players are squeezing the racket too tight. It's better to be softer with your hand and smooth instead of overhitting."* He further noted: *"You want to be like an artist painting."*

Another "trick" that can be helpful is to squeeze your grip as tightly as you can during a changeover, and then feel the sensation of your arm and hand relaxing after releasing the squeeze. Of course, you can also do this before the match starts if you are feeling overly tense.

During matches, when you start to feel your body getting tight or choking due to the pressure, deep breathing between points and changeovers can be very helpful. To fully benefit from deep breathing to slow yourself down, it's important to practice this outside of match play (I'll cover this later in the book).

Other strategies that can work are positive self-talk, simply focusing on the ball (if you are focusing on the ball, it can help distract you from negative thoughts) or focusing on the tactics you want to deploy to win the next point.

#6: Not respecting your opponent's game (a.k.a.; taking your opponent too lightly)

"I fear no one, but respect everyone."—Roger Federer

"I am never too confident. I always respect every opponent."—Rafael Nadal

Imagine stepping on the court and see an opponent with awkward looking strokes and a 70 mile-per-hour serve, and you immediately think to yourself "no way am I losing to this guy". If you are like me, you've probably played against your share of "pushers". While it's good to feel confident you will win, it is not helpful to be over-confident.

I have witnessed and experienced on many occasions the unorthodox opponent who slices and dices, gives you no pace, hits lots of drop shots, etc. When you play an opponent like this it can be easy to get frustrated because you are not able to play the way you are most comfortable. Before you know it, you may start tensing up and find yourself losing the match.

Don't fall into this trap. Show respect for your opponent from the outset, and don't put added pressure on yourself by thinking how embarrassing it would be to lose to such an "inferior" player. Successful players dig deeper and are generally able to find ways to problem-solve by making their opponents feel equally uncomfortable by exploiting their weaknesses. You may discover, for example, that your opponent is uncomfortable at the net or doesn't like to be pulled out wide.

If you find yourself losing to an opponent you think you should beat (or someone else thinks you should beat), you may get ahead of yourself and start thinking how embarrassing it would be if you were to lose the match. You may also start making excuses and mentally quitting by having thoughts like *"I hate playing guys that give me no pace"*. It's important that you stay in the present (don't get ahead of yourself) and do your best to problem solve the situation. If you are persistent and resourceful, you'll likely find some tactics that work.

Good coaches should remember not to put added pressure on their players to win when facing "inferior" opponents. Instead, they should encourage their players to respect all opponents regardless of their match record, ranking and stroke mechanics.

#7: Destructive self-talk

"When you get down on yourself—start beating yourself up mentally—there are now two players on the court trying to take you down. And one of them is you."—Brad Gilbert

"When you berate yourself and don't stop, and you get so uptight and beat the shit out of yourself, it is really hard to focus on the next point."—Paul Annacone

How many times have you been around tennis courts and overheard comments like "I can't hit a bleeping ball", "I stink today" or worse? You've probably uttered such comments yourself. This can quickly become a self-fulfilling prophesy. Before you know it, your play gets progressively worse and the match gets out of hand in a hurry.

Making negative self-comments and judgments are bad enough. Don't worsen the problem by letting your opponent hear your negative commentary. Your "meltdown" will only add fuel to his/her confidence. From personal experience, when I witness my opponent berating himself, my confidence increases, and I know the match is mine for the taking.

When you catch yourself being self-critical, remind yourself that it is only natural to make mistakes. When I make bad unforced errors, I immediately tell myself "next point" or "right here right now" to do my best to stay positive and present. The more accepting you are of yourself and your shortcomings, the easier it is to stay in the moment and give yourself the best chance to play your best tennis. It's not always easy to use productive self-talk in pressure situations, so it helps to practice it both on and off the court. I'll cover additional recommendations related to self-talk later in this book.

#8: Not able to move on (after losing a big game, getting a bad call, etc.)

"I never look back, I look forward."—Steffi Graf

"The next point - that's all you must think about."—Rod Laver

See if you can relate to this situation. You are serving at 5-4, and up 40 Love. Then you miss a couple of relatively easy shots and go on to lose the game and set. Several games later, you are still thinking about how you "blew your opportunity".

Champions like Roger Federer and Carlos Alcaraz benefit from having poor short-term memory. Having the ability to forget, regroup and move on quickly is a valuable asset for tennis players. If you think about it, one of the great things about tennis (unlike golf) is that after you make a bad shot or play a bad game, it all starts over again. Conversely, if you hit a golf ball into a bunker, you'll need to play your way out of trouble. Remember to always keep your focus on the present (the next point), and not the past (the shot you have missed) or the future (whether you will win or lose the game, set or match).

Another common reason for not being able to mentally move on is when you think (or know for a fact!) your opponent has given you a bad line call. I recall one match when my opponent called a ball out that I could clearly see was in by six inches! I got so angry I could barely play for the next couple of games, which is precisely what my opponent wanted to happen. Earlier in the match he had given me the benefit of the doubt on a couple of close line calls. To this day, I believe he was consciously setting me up for a bad call on a critical point late in the match. That match taught me a better strategy would have been to ask for a line judge, regroup, and then take out my anger and frustration on my opponent! It also taught me to work on keeping my cool, so I'll be ready when I receive highly questionable line calls.

Whenever something bad or unwanted happens, the best response is to refuse to get sucked in to anger, frustration or panic. If you do get sucked in, nine out of ten times it will negatively impact your performance on the next point or series of points. Dr. Jim Afremow, sports psychologist, suggests that you make a commitment prior to your match that you will do your best to take whatever happens out there in stride. This will help you to stay cool and confident.

It's also common to lose your focus or present orientation by having your mind be preoccupied with things that have happened in the recent or not so recent past. For example, you might step up to serve out the set and your mind reverts to how you performed the last time you attempted to serve out the set – good or bad. Or, you may still be hung up on a bone head decision you just made in the previous point.

Peter Smith (legendary coach of 5-time NCAA champion USC men's tennis teams) is a strong proponent of flipping this mindset by consciously reacting positively to your mistakes. He pointed out: *"if you have a bad reaction to them (mistakes), the chances of repeating those mistakes are going to keep increasing and increasing."* He further noted: *"At the end of the day, you are in control of how you react when things go wrong. As tough as that is when you miss an easy volley or an overhead or an easy forehand or whatever, you have to have the correct mindset so you can do the right things going forward."*

One of the key items we'll also cover more in depth is what you can do to stay present-oriented, so your mind doesn't drift to what has happened in the past or what could potentially happen in the future. Being able to maintain a present-orientation takes practice, and is critical to gaining and sustaining a mental edge.

#9: Losing focus

"I play each point like my life depends on it."—Rafael Nadal

"If you can keep playing tennis when somebody is shooting a gun down the street, that's concentration."—Serena Williams

Winning tennis requires being able to maintain good concentration and focus. On numerous occasions I've seen players get distracted by what is happening on other courts, things going on in their lives off the courts, spectators who are cheering or booing, babies crying, cars driving by, etc. To perform your best, you need to be able to block out such distractions.

On one occasion, I recall playing an opponent in a USTA match who revealed in the warm up he had an important appointment later that afternoon. When the match went longer than he expected, it became clear he was worrying about arriving late for his appointment.

Although it can be difficult to be totally focused on your match when you have other things on your mind, successful players are generally good at compartmentalizing by blocking out other thoughts and distractions. It's also not a good idea to reveal to your opponent you have other important things on your mind!

Sometimes bigger distractions such as life events can cause us to lose focus. To a certain degree, everything in our life is interconnected in some way. If things are crumbling all around us in our personal lives, our tennis game is likely to suffer. Conversely, when everything feels right in our personal lives, this can have a positive impact on our ability to relax and enjoy the fun and competition that tennis can bring and play our best.

It is not uncommon for top pros to have setbacks on their ranking and performance due to major outside distractions such as marriage breakups, death of a parent or coach, significant injuries, etc. It's only human. In some cases, to be able to perform your best may even require taking some time away or possibly counseling (including grief counseling) so you can regroup and re-focus on your tennis and not be consumed by life events.

#10: Playing the excuse game

"I just try to play tennis and don't find excuses. You know, I just lost because I lost, not because my arm was sore."—Goran Ivanisevic, former Wimbledon champion

"Never has an excuse made us win a match."—Toni Nadal, coach of Rafael Nadal

"The courts are too slow (or fast), my opponent is getting lucky, it's too windy, it's too hot, my shoulder is sore, etc." These are just a few of the literally hundreds of excuses tennis players have for playing poorly and losing matches. When I hear my opponent starting to make excuses it gives me that much more confidence I will win the match. It often indirectly implies my game is getting to him.

After anger and frustration, excuse-making is probably the most wide-spread method of escape from the stress and uncertainty of competition according to Dr. Allen Fox, psychologist and former tennis pro. If you feel an excuse coming on, try to push it to the back of your mind and get down to the business of trying to win the match. The urge to "escape" from the stress by making excuses or getting frustrated is high, so a lot of discipline may be required.

Playing the excuse game definitely won't help you win. In fact, making excuses can be a self-fulfilling prophesy, and can easily lead to tanking (i.e., quitting to keep your self-esteem intact). Instead, try to convince yourself that you'll find a way to win the match no matter what the obstacle or situation. If you are way behind, say 5-1, if you are able to win a game or two, your opponent will very likely start to feel the pressure of trying to close out the set or match. Mentally tough players rarely make excuses for losing. Instead of making excuses, it can be helpful to focus on little wins, like telling yourself *"I'm going to win the next point or next game."*

If you do end up losing the match, don't make excuses. By blaming our equipment, bad weather, luck, etc., we only cushion the blow to our egos by making ourselves believe we did the best we could. In doing so, we rob ourselves of the learning opportunity presented to us. It also makes us look weak and like a bad sport to our opponents and others.

Darrin Donnelly, author of "Victory Favors the Fearless", pointed out: *"There are two types of people in this world: Those who believe success is a choice and those who make excuses for why they're not successful."*

Allon Khakshouri talks about how tennis players may self-sabotage as a way to justify why they lose in *"The Ultimate Guide to Becoming a Mentally Tough Tennis Player."* He explains: *"they may party the night before a big match and/or portray an image of not caring. By doing so, "a tennis player can eliminate pressure: If they lose, they have an excuse. They didn't practice, felt ill, or partied all night long. However, if they do find a way to win, they become superheroes who can beat their competitors despite their poor preparations."*

He refers to this as a classical win-win situation. *"The real purpose of self-sabotaging behaviors is quite simple: They justify failures! In fact, one of the worst forms of self-sabotaging behaviors happens when we make up excuses, often even before playing a match."* In actuality, self-sabotaging behaviors prevent us from giving our best effort and impede our efforts to maximize our performance over time.

#11: Playing not to lose

"I can live with losing, I can't live without taking my chance."—Andre Agassi

The worst feeling I ever had on the tennis court was a college match that I lost after being up 5-0 in a close out set. By the time my opponent fought back, and we had reached 5-4, I had lost all momentum, and felt like I could do nothing right, and it seemed like my opponent could not miss.

What did I do to blow that set and ultimately the match? Part of it, was that I had gotten too conservative. Instead of staying aggressive and looking to close out points, I allowed my opponent to find his groove. Also, each game my opponent won, I lost more and more confidence. This was then followed by me playing the "what if" game in my mind. In other words, I started thinking, what if I were to lose this set after being up 5-0? How will I explain that to my teammates and coach? Of course, that just made me more nervous and anxious and lose my focus.

Momentum is a funny thing in sports. You can literally feel a match slipping away if you get caught up in it. The best way to approach these situations is to do your best to remain calm, present and positive. Try to slow down and not rush your shots and do everything in your power to make your opponent earn all points by keeping the pressure on him. The hardest point to win is often the last one. The clock never runs out in tennis matches! You need to close out the match.

It's also somewhat natural to relax a bit and take the foot off the pedal when you get a big lead. Craig O'Shannessy talks about how it is a fairly common phenomenon to get tight and have a difficult time closing out matches. He noted: *"We tend to focus on the finish line, which is not where we want our mind to be."* He suggests saying something like this to yourself on the changeovers: *"Long way to go, keep working"*. This can help to redirect your mind to stay in the present, and not look ahead.

O'Shannessy further noted: *"What matters is how you choose to focus your mind when you are in these challenging moments."* Can you settle down and narrow your focus on your tactics and targets? Are you willing to hit through the ball and not be a victim of your frustration and anger? If we don't panic, stick to what had been working earlier in the match and stay in the present, we stand a much better chance of closing out the match when our opponent starts to gain momentum.

#12: Dwelling on your losses (instead of learning from them)

"Losing is only temporary and not all encompassing. You must simply study it, learn from it, and try hard not to lose the same way again. Then you must have the self-control to forget about it."—John Wooden, legendary college basketball coach at UCLA

"I really think a champion is defined not by their wins, but by how they can recover when they fall."—Serena Williams

I'd bet John McEnroe would like to have another crack at that 1984 French Open Final he lost to Ivan Lendl after leading two sets to none. He never made it back to the Finals of that Grand Slam event again. On the flip side, how did number 1 ranked Ivan Lendl manage to lose the French Open semifinals to a cramping, under-hand serving 17-year-old kid named Michael Chang in 1989?

All pros and competitive players have suffered defeats when they were expected to win or in position to win. It's part of the game. However, if you can learn a lesson from those defeats, you will be in a better position when faced with a similar situation in the future.

It's beneficial to experience the pain and emotions associated with losing, and then to quickly refocus so you don't lose confidence. Sometimes a painful loss can be just what's needed to show you where your game still needs to improve and motivate you to take your game and training to the next level.

On some occasions it can be difficult to pinpoint the exact reasons for losing a close match. In fact, there can be multiple issues at play. Examples include: you got tight, your opponent got hot, your fitness level caused your play to progressively get worse, etc. If possible, have a coach or a teammate observe your matches, so you can compare notes after each match.

As legendary coach, John Wooden, noted in the quote above, having a short-term memory to not dwell on your defeats is beneficial. We should accept that we will lose some matches (even the top pros lose several times a year), and learn from it, but that doesn't mean we should lose sleep or our confidence when we lose.

People who are very successful in life will often tell you their definition of success is their response to failure, and they would argue that you have to have failures to learn how to win. In other words, there's no such thing as success without experiencing failure (source: "A Sports Psychologist Reveals the Secrets to a Powerful Mindset", Forbes, April 5, 2017). If as tennis players we can accept that losing is a natural and inevitable part of our lives as athletes, it will free us up to perform with confidence, commitment, and courage rather than worry, doubt, and anxiety.

Amber McGinnis, a highly ranked junior in Florida, says she has worked on turning the page and moving on after losses. "*I have learned to stay calm and talk it over with my coach and that will be it.*" Further, she noted that when she gets back to practice the next day, she'll work on not making the same mistakes again, whether they were her tactics, attitude, footwork, etc. Losing also tends to make her motivated to work that much harder on her fitness.

Think about it. What's one thing successful tennis players (especially top pros) do better than just about everyone else? Answer: they don't take failure personally.

"*You have to want to win and do your best. But once you enter the match, you need to detach from the outcome. You need to remember that life is much bigger than a tennis game. Remember, 'It's only a tennis game, and all I want is to do my best and try to win point for point. And then, if I win, great. And if I lose, I'll have amazing feedback.'*" (Source: "I managed the world's best tennis players. Here's what I learned about being a top performer", by Katie Parrott).

"*Make no mistake: this paradox — of doing absolutely everything in your power to play the best game you can, but at the same time not letting yourself be absolutely destroyed if your best isn't enough — is a tough one to grasp. But it's the paradox we all should learn to get comfortable with, whether we're trying to be top tennis players — or top performers in any field.*"

Remember, we are not defined by what happens to us. **We are defined by how we *respond* to what happens to us.**

#13: Viewing competition as a threat, not a challenge

"Fear is part of my life and career. For me it is a big engine, it's something that helps me getting up in the morning and achieving goals. Without fear, I wouldn't be here."—Matteo Berrettini

"I learned in my life that you have to accept it (pressure), you can't ignore it. It's going to be there. You feel it. So, instead of trying to say, "I'm not nervous," I'm saying, "I am nervous, I do feel pressure, I do feel this." "Once you acknowledge a problem, you can solve it."—Coco Gauff

"I just like the fight."—Petra Kvitova

According to Jim Taylor, PhD, (*"Six Attitudes Parents Should Instill in Their Young Athletes"*, Psychology Today, Jan 08, 2019), a simple distinction appears to lie at the heart of whether athletes are able to rise to the occasion and perform their best when it really counts or crumble under the weight of expectations and tough conditions on the day of a competition: Do they view the competition as a threat or a challenge.

Dr. Jim Loehr defines the *"challenge response"* as when the player can still give 100% effort when the pressure is on and remain completely positive and play without fear. **The challenge response is the bullseye of mental toughness**. It is learned, and it must be practiced over and over.

On the other hand, what happens when athletes approach a competition as a threat? Physiologically, their muscles tighten up, their breathing gets shallow and their balance starts to suffer. Psychologically, their motivation is to flee from the threat. Their confidence plummets. Emotionally, they feel fear, helplessness, and despair. In sum, everything both physically and mentally goes against athletes, making it virtually impossible to overcome the threat and find success in their sport. Where does the threat come from? Most powerfully, from a fear of failure.

According to Anne Grady, author of "Mind Over Moment: Harness the Power of Resilience," when you are fearful, your innovative and creative brain shuts down (source: The Resilience Reset with Anne Grady – Dr. Cindra Kamphoff Podcast, 2020). As a tennis player, that makes it very difficult for you to strategically problem solve what you need to do to give yourself the best chance to win.

A "challenge" reaction produces an entirely different set of responses. Physiologically, athletes are fired up, but also relaxed, with just the right amount of adrenaline to make them feel strong, quick, and fast. Muscles are loose, breathing is steady, and balance is centered. Psychologically, athletes' singular motivation is to overcome the challenge. They are confident that they can surmount the challenges of the competition. They are laser-focused on the challenge before them. As for emotions, they feel excitement, inspiration, pride, and courage. In sum, their entire physical and psychological being is directed toward triumphing over the challenge and their chances of finding success are high. **The important thing for athletes to understand is that threat vs. challenge is all in their minds, about how they perceive it.**

Athletes with a challenge reaction do not have a fear of failure and are solely driven to perform their best to pursue the successful achievement of their goals. These athletes are focused on:

- Improving
- Giving their best effort
- Going all out
- Having fun
- Making progress toward their goals

Not surprisingly, when tennis players (or any athletes) are focused on pursuing success or excellence rather than avoiding failure, they are more likely to perform well and achieve better results. As covered earlier, if your mind is focused on winning or losing, a challenge mindset is basically impossible to achieve. I would add, if your motivation to win (or avoid losing) is not to let others down, you will not be able to achieve a challenge mindset.

#14: Not following a mental and physical pre-match routine

"I think it all starts even before you get on the court, and what you do to get yourself mentally prepared for the match and get yourself in the right state of mind where you are calm, composed and serene enough, but yet you have the right intensity and the drive and motivation to play well."—Novak Djokovic

Tennis players like other athletes tend to be creatures of habit. Not following a pre-match routine can easily take you out of your comfort zone. Without a consistent pre-match routine, you will likely put yourself at a disadvantage before the match gets started. For example, it's always important to drink sufficient water (or energy drink of choice) before and during your match to stay hydrated to play your best. Also, eat a nutritious pre-match meal a couple of hours before matches. Your pre-match routine should also cover ensuring your racquets are strung properly and you have all the other equipment you may need (such as a grip change, towel and hat).

Brad Gilbert, in his book "Winning Ugly", talked about how he uses a checklist to make sure he has everything he could possibly need to give himself the best chance to win. He noted: "*I don't want to even take the slightest chance that a blister, a cramp, dehydration, hunger, broken rackets, strings, sweaty socks or grips, shoelaces, or anything else could affect my ability to win. I don't leave anything to chance.*"

Whether you are a creature of habit or not, you should do whatever is necessary to arrive at your matches fully prepared and confident. The only person you cannot deceive is yourself!

Using a timeline can be an excellent tool to enable you to be fully prepared and confident. Take back your timeline as far as required to ensure you are getting the proper nutrition, hydration and sleep leading up to the match.

In preparation for matches, you can also try to release some of the pressure on yourself by setting personal goals around what you can control. You cannot control how others perform. The goal should always be to prepare and perform to your best and deliver the best you. Your results will always be influenced by your preparation.

One element I mentioned earlier in this book is the importance of managing your expectations coming into each match. On one extreme you can be overconfident, which can be very dangerous because it is natural to begin to panic at the first sign of adversity. At the other extreme, is to have little self-belief you can beat your opponent due to previous matches, his ranking, his reputation, etc. In this case, you may go in thinking "What's the point of trying since I'm going to get crushed anyway."

A better approach going into each match is to tell yourself *"I'll do whatever it takes to fight to win this match."* (Source, Essential Tennis, Ian Westerman). Go in being fully cognizant that you can't control everything that will happen. In fact, all you really can control is your level of focus, intensity, and effort. Try to stay in the moment on each shot and each point throughout the match and do your best to not worry about the outcome (good or bad).

Immediately before a match, what's the best way to get your mind and body ready to compete to the best of your ability? I asked this question to a number of former pros, coaches, top juniors and former college players. Here's some of what they had to say:

- Visualize the game plan and the sequences/patterns of play you want to use.
- Talk with your coach (if available) to remind yourself what you want to do regardless of how the match progresses (examples include performance goals, rituals, deep breaths, etc.).
- Arrive at least 30 minutes to an hour before you play. If possible, warm up with a partner or hit against the wall.
- Meditate and/or breathe deeply for 5 to 10 minutes on your own.

- Listen to music – either to get yourself more relaxed or more pumped up. Experiment to see what works best for you.

#15: Your game and conditioning need work

"Nothing can substitute for just plain hard work."—Andre Agassi

"I made it look so easy on court all those years. No one realized how hard I had to work. No one realized how much I had to put into it."—Pete Sampras

If you want to achieve peak performance, it's extremely important to put in the work both on and off the court to take your game and results to the next level. I've observed many talented players who appear unwilling to put in the work and training required to improve their fitness and gain a competitive edge. To reach your potential, talent alone won't get you there. You need to put in the time and effort to groove your strokes and achieve a high level of mental and physical fitness.

The hotter and more humid the playing conditions, the more critical your physical fitness becomes for sustaining a high level of performance over a long match, and a potentially much longer tournament. Sometimes, tournaments require you to play multiple matches on a single day, and in these situations your fitness level will very likely impact your results. If you are like me, you hate for your play to suffer due to your fitness. I've suffered muscle cramps, for example, on hot, humid days. Which reminds me of a recent USTA match when my body started cramping up badly in the third set tiebreaker. Even if I won the match, I would have had to play a second match later that day and I knew there was no way I could physically do it. That was a very disappointing way to be knocked out of a tournament!

Ask yourself: do I consistently put in the on-court time to drill and improve my overall fitness and performance? Or, do I skip the hard work and jump into playing practice sets after only a brief warm up? To continue to improve and reach higher levels of performance you need to be willing to put in the extra work that makes you uncomfortable. Winners get up out of bed and don't make excuses on those days when they are feeling lazy, tired, or sore.

In addition, the fitter you get, the better you will move on the court. If your movement improves then you can set up your shots correctly. And once the ball comes back, you'll be ready for more.

As George Mumford, author of "The Mindful Athlete", pointed out, *"every high-performing mindful athlete knows that if you want to achieve something, there's a good chance you can, but only if you are willing to pay the price. You have to be committed to doing the same things thousands and thousands of times with intention."* Further, *"you have to practice that thing over and over again deliberately, which means with concentrated focus, steadiness of mind, intention, and a willingness to push yourself out of your comfort zone."*

In addition to putting in the hard work, it's important to set high personal standards. Tony Robbins, motivational speaker, noted: when we raise our standards and achieve a higher level of dedication, we stop saying *"I should"* and start saying *'I will."* As a bonus, if we know we have put in the hard work, it also tends to increase our confidence and self-belief.

If you are a serious player and are motivated to do everything you can to improve your game, it's also critical to gain self-awareness of what you need to work on to take your game to the next level. Is your service motion holding you back? Does your slice backhand invite your opponent to attack you? Does your forehand tend to go astray on big points?

There may be several flaws in your game that could be addressed, however, often there are one or two simple things you can focus on in practice to significantly improve your game.

How do you decide what to work on? I've found the most effective way to raise your self-awareness and address the fundamental flaws in your game is via video feedback. If you haven't had the opportunity to view and study video feedback of yourself, you may be shocked by what you see! It really is a game changer that will help to raise your awareness and pinpoint what needs work. I can't emphasize this enough. Without using video feedback, you are simply guessing what you need to work on.

Armed with video feedback and increased self-awareness, your next step is to incorporate one or two simple adjustments to improve your stroke mechanics. You can then use your practice sessions to focus on these areas to take advantage of your increased self-awareness.

Another great way to raise your self-awareness is via coaching feedback. Of course, not all coaches are created equal. Choosing a coach can be a personal and complicated matter. I believe the most important factor in selecting a coach is to go with someone you fully trust and believe in. If you are lucky to have a coach you fully trust, you will also be more likely to enjoy the process that goes into improving your game.

In the book "The Best Tennis of Your Life," Jeff Greenwald suggests choosing your coach wisely. More specifically, before committing to a coach, it's helpful to ask about his/her philosophy of coaching. He also noted: *"When a coach lectures too much and doesn't ask if what you are doing feels right or makes sense, this is a sign that you may be going down the wrong road."*

Almost everyone wants (or hopes for) a quick fix and instant results, but improving your game is typically a process that requires patience and hard work.

Ultimately, you want to grow as a player to become self-aware of how to improve your mental game, strokes and strategy. Or, as Andre Agassi noted: *"A great coach can lead you to a place where you don't need him anymore."*

#16: You don't make your opponent earn the big points

"The experience of playing so many tough matches, close matches where it's decided on one or two points down the stretch helps me to cope with those pressure moments."—Novak Djokovic

"I think it's the mark of a great player to be confident in tough situations."—John McEnroe

"I think with the scoring system in tennis, certain points are more important than others. I think the best players tend to focus in more and make better decisions, less mistakes and they sort of up their games and their intensity in those moments."—Andy Murray

In many highly competitive matches, a few key points can swing the momentum and determine who comes out on top. In general, however, it is best to treat all points as important, but no point (even match point!) too important. That will help you to keep your emotions on an even keel. Nonetheless, I believe there are some tactics you should consider when playing big points, like break points on your serve.

First, are you truly making your opponent earn the big points? For example, are you prone to over-hitting and giving your opponent free points when it matters most? Conversely, do you play too conservatively on break points and/or close out points? Do you sometimes abandon a winning game plan or become more tentative when trying to close out a match?

So, how do you make your opponent earn critical points? One way is to get your first serve in by going with your most consistent serve, the one that has been doing the most damage in the match. To do that, you need to pay attention to what has been working for you, and what your opponent has been struggling with. Conversely, if you are the returner, your focus can be to return the ball deep to your opponent's weaker side.

It's also helpful to pay attention to your opponent's body language. For example, if your opponent has just mishit an easy forehand, and you can easily see his or her frustration after missing the shot, why not serve to the forehand in the next big point?

Another strategy I've had some success with is surprising my opponent by serve and volleying on a key point. This strategy tends to be most effective when your opponent has been slicing most of his return of serves and/or returning defensively. It's also generally a good strategy to come in to the net when your opponent hits a short ball to put pressure on him. After all, if you don't follow short balls into the net, it sends your opponent a message that he won't have to pay or get punished when he hits short balls.

Amber McGinnis, a highly ranked player from Florida, says she likes to apply pressure on her opponents, especially when her opponents have a second serve on big points. *"I move in and show them I am loose and try to control the point from the outset."* On the other hand, she also believes when it's late in the third set it's important to play consistently, by building the point, and waiting for the best opportunity to step forward and attack.

The main takeaway is that you should make your opponent earn key points by keeping the pressure on him or her, and not giving the point away yourself. How you do this should be predicated by what you are doing well and have confidence in, and by paying attention to what your opponent has been struggling with throughout the match.

#17: Throwing in the towel when you're not playing your best

"I always say, you have to believe in yourself. Hope is the last thing that you lose."—Carlos Alcaraz

"What is the single most important quality in a tennis champion? I would have to say desire, staying in there and winning matches when you are not playing that well."—John McEnroe

"The great part about tennis is you can't run out the clock…. As long as we we're still playing, I had a chance."—Andre Agassi

"Never give up. Because great things take time."— Dominic Thiem

Simply put, if you want to win more matches, you can never quit. As Agassi's quote states well, there is no clock in tennis. Until your opponent wins the match, you always have a chance. It may be a slim chance on your worst day (or your opponent's best day), but there is always the possibility that you can find lightening in a bottle with a new approach or tactics, your opponent can start to feel the pressure and play worse or he can run out of gas and/or get injured.

Tennis is a sport where some days you are playing great and other days you are playing way below your capability. There are only a few things you can control regardless of how you are hitting the ball; they are: staying intense, moving your feet, preparing properly for the match and, perhaps most importantly, your thought process during the match. An average player would think during a match, on an "off day", that today is just not my day and throw in the towel. Conversely, a mentally tough player will understand that he is not playing his best but will still do everything he can to win the match.

When you are not having your best day, tell yourself you will remain positive, confident and resilient. If nothing you are doing seems to be working, don't stop fighting and do keep your feet moving. Also, try different tactics, shot selections, changes of pace, etc. After all, what have you got to lose? Remember, the pressure is on your opponent to close out the match.

#18: Failing to maintain a positive mind and body language between points and games

"The only thing you have control over is your attitude." —Rick Macci, Hall-of-Fame coach

Are you able to maintain the right balance of relaxed concentration and intensity throughout your matches? Most of us will struggle to do this at various stages throughout matches.

One mental trick to winning more matches is to simply be able to pump yourself up when you are feeling deflated. Although how you feel can affect your body language, the reverse is also true, as a change in your body language can affect how you feel. When you feel your energy level dropping, try emphasizing positive body language by puffing your chest out and smiling between points. As a bonus, it will send a message to your opponent that he is not getting to you! Check out the video, *"Tennis Mental Trick Win More Matches (Top Speed Tennis)"*, for more details on body language and its impact on your energy level.

Dr. Jim Loehr believes what you do between points reveals quite a bit about how mentally tough you are. The good news is that you can learn to manage the time between points by training to increase your mental toughness. He refers to this as "The 16-Second Cure", and if done properly, it can help players master the challenge response we covered earlier.

According to Loehr, there are 4 activities or "stages" the mentally tough player completes between points:

1. Positive physical response – the player's walk is high energy with chest out. The racquet may move to the non-dominant hand to provide rest. The image is strong, powerful, and confident. The player may pump his fist after a particularly good shot, or clap for an opponent's great shot. No negative emotions are projected immediately after they make a mistake. Or, as Dr. Allen Fox points out: *"The trick in maximizing performance is for players to produce positive emotions before every point, independent of what is happening on the court."* (Source: "Tennis: Winning the Mental Match").

2. Relaxation – look at one's strings to facilitate the "relaxation response". The player allows time for their breathing and heart rate to stabilize, especially after a physically demanding point. Their arms and hands stay relaxed and free.

3. Preparation – this is when the player moves to the baseline to begin to serve or to get in position to return serve. They lift their eyes and look at their opponent's side of the court. They typically make a strong statement with their physical bodies again as if to say: *"I will win this point."* It is essentially programming your mind to what you want to do before you start the point.

4. Rituals – the rituals immediately before the next point help to deepen concentration and will vary from player to player. The server will bounce the

ball at least two times and will pause before beginning the service motion to help prevent him from speeding up the service motion due to being under pressure. The returner will get physically ready by jumping up and down and/or being on his toes. Both server and receiver should be visualizing what they want to do as far as the serve or return, with no focus on other matters such as strategy or tactics. The goal is to play instinctively and automatically.

For more details on these four stages, reference video "The 16-Second Cure with Dr. Jim Loehr". Dr. Loehr also talks about the importance of athletes getting to their "Ideal Performance State" or IPS in his book, "The New Mental Toughness Training for Sports." This is what coach Brett Kurtz refers to as the optimal arousal level. A key way to reach your IPS is to use rituals to pump yourself up when your energy is low.

Dr. Loehr also believes that "positive brainwashing" can be used to train your brain to be more confident on the court. He suggests you pick the weakest element of your game (for example, your second serve) and write down the opposite of how you feel about it. If you think "My second serve is weak", you could write down "I have a great second serve" or "I love hitting second serves." Not only should you write this down, but you should post it all over the place – in your house, on your computer, in your tennis bag, etc. This is essentially the same concept that Jeff Salzenstein, former top 100 pro, was referring to when he spoke to me about rewiring your unconscious mind. You want to essentially change the language you use to associate about yourself and your game. Try it out. It's powerful stuff!

#19: Lack of consistency

"It's difficult to maintain the level I showed at the start (of the match), few players are capable of it." —Felix Auger-Aliassime

This may sound simplistic, but an overlooked tactic to winning more matches is plain, old consistency. If your opponent can only hit about 5 shots before making an error, be more consistent by making at least 6 shots! You don't need to go for big winners or aces to win in tennis. Often, the more consistent player is the one who wins the match. The "deadly sin" is going for too much on your shots, especially at the start of each point, making unforced errors that hand your opponent the point.

I remember an important match in my junior playing days when my opponent had found a groove and was taking advantage of my unforced errors. I was confident I had the ability to be more patient and consistent than my opponent, so I decided to change tactics by making him earn more points by consistently hitting deep down the middle of the court. This simple change in tactics caused my opponent to significantly increase his unforced errors, and I was able to pull away and easily win the third set. As the late, great Vic Braden noted, *"you can win 33% more points by getting just one more ball back."*

Research has also shown that the majority of points for advanced players (NTRP level 4.5 and higher) last only a few shots. In fact, 70% of all points are between one and four shots, with many points won with only one or two shots. Since points tend to be very short in highly competitive tennis, it's extremely important to work to improve your skills and consistency as a server and returner. As the server, you need to have a reliable enough spin on your second serve, so your opponents have to earn points and you don't make it easy for them to attack you or worse off, give points away by double faulting.

Assuming the rally does get to a third or fourth shot, it's generally a good tactic to aim to be consistent with your shots (that is, don't go for more than necessary) that immediately follow the serve and return, since your opponent is likely to give you a fair percentage of unforced errors if you employ that tactic. Be careful with this tactic, though since there is a fine line between trying to be consistent and not hitting through the ball and going for your targets. The idea is to not overhit and spray balls all over the court. On a related point, advanced players need to also be competent at attacking short balls with effective, consistent approach shots and finishing points at the net via volleys and overheads.

Consistency is also very important when you are playing a stronger player. It's easy to think we have to go for everything to compete with a stronger player. Remember not to go for shots you wouldn't normally hit, just because you are playing a "better" or more highly ranked player. Essentially, you will end up handing the other player the match the vast majority of the time. Of course, you should not hold back when the opportunity presents itself for a winning or attacking shot that you are capable of making 3 out of 4 times.

#20: Lack of a game plan (not playing to your strengths and your opponent's weaknesses)

"Winning tennis is as much about problem-solving and adversity management as it is about forehands and backhands."—Justin Gimelstob, former ATP Professional

Having an initial game plan will help you be more effective than not having one. Sounds pretty basic, but I've seen many players who try to outhit their opponents, and don't seem to have any idea or plan for what they want to do. In other words, they have a low tennis IQ. An important benefit to having a game plan is that it focuses your brain more on execution than stroke mechanics or the outcome (i.e., whether you will win or lose).

A basic game plan typically calls for trying to exploit your opponent's weaknesses while playing to your own strengths. Playing to your opponent's weakness (low or high backhands are common examples) is generally a good strategy for opening up the court or generating a weak reply which you can use to get your opponent on the run or to end the point.

On a related note, if your forehand is your strength, the odds are in your favor if you are using your forehand to attack your opponent's weaker side. Remember though, it may not be as simple as which side is weaker. By paying attention to the points, you should be able to discern if high balls or low balls give your opponent more problems, as well as whether deep balls, wide balls or short balls create more opportunities for you to play to your strengths and win points more easily.

A key element to executing your game plan is knowing how to construct points. According to former ATP player and current coach, Todd Widom, not knowing how to properly construct points holds players back from taking their game and their results to the next level. Widom believes if you are not looking to construct proper points, that likely means you have no game plan, which is a recipe for poor or inconsistent results.

Widom noted that there are two common patterns to constructing points:

The "2 and 1" pattern – hit 2 shots to the backhand (or weaker side) and then open up the court with your third shot.

The "1 and 1" pattern – alternate hitting from one side to the other. This can be good strategy when your opponent has poor mobility and/or has sub-par conditioning, since you are getting them to move the whole time.

Widom also has his students practice the serve plus one pattern (use your serve to open up the court for your second shot). For example, serve to the tee in the deuce court, anticipate a return down the middle or down the line, and then hit a backhand or inside out forehand to the open court to take control of the point.

Another good tactic is to pay attention to your opponent's game to figure out what his weakest shot is and go to it over and over. Their weakest shot is likely to break down in the most important moments of the match when the points and games are more critical.

Another way of looking at it is to pay attention to what is working and stay with it. If you are winning 2 out of 3 points with your basic game plan, don't go away from it when you lose a point. It takes confidence to maintain your game plan and pattern of play when it doesn't always work out every time. It also takes discipline to stay with a pattern of play and utilize it over and over again.

Widom believes it takes a lot of discipline to consistently execute a pattern of play throughout a match. He noted that you can't have mental lapses where you are hitting the ball too passively and too short in the court and "inviting" your opponent to attack you. That won't work as you get to higher level tennis. He, like Jeff Salzenstein, believe that *"tennis is about hitting targets."* Widom noted: *"If you can hit your targets 3 or 4 times in a row consistently, you can develop into a highly accomplished player."* He also talked about the importance of working on your pattern of play every day, so you don't have to think about it when you are in a tournament. He noted that it comes down to discipline of training which can be taught by a coach.

He believes that self-confidence may need to be developed for juniors (and others) to execute and stick with a pattern of play. He talked about how if you are scared to miss, your self-confidence will need to be developed to be willing to hit out more aggressively – this is typically required when juniors move up in level (for example, from 14 and under to 16 and under). You need to be able to load up and accelerate on your groundstrokes. Conversely, some players may need to learn to tone down their aggressiveness to be more consistent in hitting their targets.

A good coach will have the player play practice sets and then stop the match as often as possible to ask the player what he did right and wrong in his hitting pattern. The coach might ask questions like: What did you do there and why? What did your opponent do that didn't allow you to execute your game plan (after you lose the point)? This is time consuming, but an effective approach for the coach to take to help the player become more self-aware and raise their tennis IQ.

Most players tend to fall back to their comfort zone in tournaments. That is, their habits will come out in the most pressure-filled situations unless they make a commitment to do otherwise (that is; sticking to a game plan while also maintaining flexibility to adjust on the fly). If your coach watches you play matches, he can help you address these issues back in practice.

Alexandra Osborne hitting a two-handed backhand drive.

Alexandra Osborne hitting a topspin forehand drive.

Jonathan Fromkin and Amber McGinnis before a practice session.

Amber McGinnis hitting a forehand volley.

Amber McGinnis hitting a serve.

Stephanie Taylor and Amber McGinnis taking a break between practice.

Jonathan Fromkin hitting a backhand volley.

Amber McGinnis hitting a two-handed backhand drive.

Coach Diego Ayala giving instruction to Eugenie Bouchard at a practice session.

Coach Diego Ayala hand-feeding balls to professional player Eugenie Bouchard.

George Bezecny, University of Georgia, hitting a forehand drive.

George Bezecny hitting a backhand.

Michelle and Samara Eisenberg practicing at Binghamton University.

Samara Eisenberg hitting a topspin forehand.

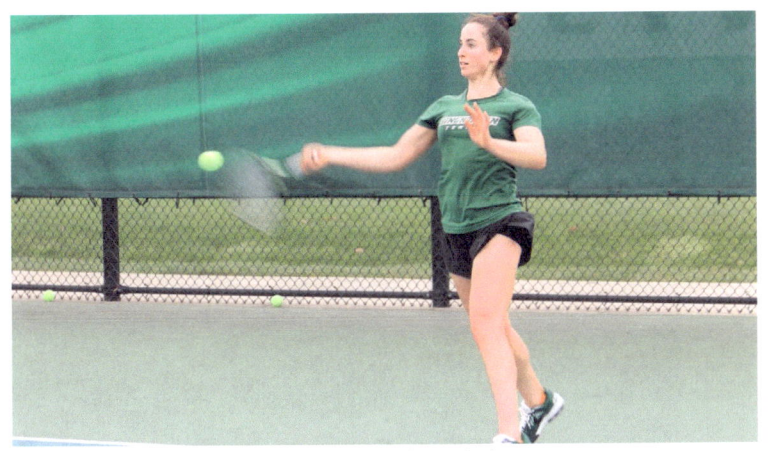

Samara Eisenberg hitting a forehand drive.

Michelle Eisenberg ready to strike a backhand return.

Jake Ly, Redlands University, prepares to hit a backhand slice return.

Jake Ly prepares to hit a backhand drive.

Jake Ly hits a serve.

Jake Ly hits a backhand return.

Alexandra Osborne and Ebony Panoho after winning the Ojai Championships PAC-12 Doubles Final for Arizona State in 2016.

Colter and Peter Smith (top row second from left) after winning the Father-Son National Championship.

Riley and Peter Smith (top row fourth from left) after winning the Father-Son National Championship.

Tanner and Peter Smith (top row fourth from left) after winning the Father-Son National Championship.

The Smith Family (from left to right) Tammie, Tanner, Peter, Riley, and Colter Smith after Tanner and Riley won the Ojai Doubles Championship.

Key character traits to becoming a winner on and off the court

"Show me a player who hits the big shot when it counts, and I'll show you courage. Everybody isn't a winner, but everybody can be a winner." – Rick Macci, Hall-of-Fame tennis coach, and former coach of Venus and Serena Williams

No matter how good you are in tennis (even if you make it on the professional tour), you are still going to have most of your life to live off the court. Therefore, you should learn to rely on yourself and not blame others when things don't go well. This is an important factor in growing and maturing as a person. According to John O'Sullivan, soccer coach and author of "Every Moment Matters", *"Cutting corners and cheating may help you win today, but eventually it will catch up with you and won't play well with the rest of your life."* O'Sullivan believes coaches should optimally collaborate with parents to help teach character to young players.

In speaking on this topic on a "Parenting Aces" podcast O'Sullivan stated: *"Our job is to not to prepare the path for the child, it's to prepare the child for the path."* One way we do this is by preparing young players for all the ups and downs and struggles that competitive sports will bring. In tennis, this is about helping players develop perseverance and the mental strength to be able to endure and overcome the mental and physical challenges they will face.

Toni Nadal, Rafael Nadal's uncle and coach, also made character development a priority. He said that he used to tell Rafael they were going to practice for an hour and half, and then he would continue the practice indefinitely to build up his strength to endure and persevere. He believes character is built up when things are difficult.

O'Sullivan acknowledges: *"There is a level of ruthlessness and selfishness to be able to train at a very high level for that long and that hard. You have to give up and sacrifice other things."* However, he also believes *"you don't have to forsake your personal development to turn into a tennis robot."* He further noted: *"If you don't develop your mental skills and character, you will likely eventually crash and burn at the highest (professional) level, and this may subject you to public humiliation."*

Brett Kurtz is also a proponent of developing character, or as he likes to call it: *"teaching life lessons through sports."* In addition to teaching players to take responsibility and accountability for changing their own behavior, he also expects his players to have the best attitude and compete hard for every point.

Jonathan Fromkin, one of Kurtz' junior players, spoke about how Kurtz has been instrumental in his development as a person and as a player: *"I've learned the importance of discipline and hard work."* Jonathan also revealed: *"I used to throw my racket in practice when I got frustrated. I haven't broken a racket in over two years now."* He also talked about how he has done a much better job of keeping his composure and continuing to fight and compete when he gets frustrated and/or is having a rough day on the court.

Kurtz believes *"many juniors and young adults are like robots, and they are used to others telling them what to do."* Further, that learning to take responsibility is an important life skill. I concur with this, because when you try to blame others, such as the coach, your opponent, the umpire, etc. or make excuses, you're only hurting yourself by not accepting your role in the outcome. The same, of course, applies to life off of the court.

Peter Scales, PhD, author of "Mental and Emotional Training for Tennis" had similar sentiments on players taking personal responsibility: *"You should think of yourself as the CEO of your tennis business. The coach is your advisor, but in the end, you make the choices."*

Toni Nadal also talked about how he put the onus and responsibility on Rafael to put in the work to become a great player. He told a story about how Rafael was once playing with a broken racket as a teenager, and after he lost, Rafael didn't blame it on the racket because it was so ingrained in him to take personal responsibility when he lost. Toni never let him get away with making any excuses, and I'm sure that contributed to Rafael's mental toughness and success.

Morgan Shepherd, tennis coach and psychologist, speaking on the "Parenting Aces" podcast, views highly competitive tennis as an excellent opportunity for personal growth and life lessons. He commented: *"Tennis is a microcosm of life." It is a practice that gives us a chance to develop ourselves. We are learning how to become more natural in life. If I give myself up to something, and am fully authentic, it takes all of us – all of our emotions – we need to be on stage and give our best. In the end, as competitive tennis players, we are opening ourselves up to the highest level of performance and satisfaction.*"

Shepherd also pointed out that tennis teaches us to maintain focus on the task at hand, in spite of internal and external obstacles such as frustration, anger, fatigue and opponents cheating. Being able to maintain focus is a key trait for achieving results on and off the court. Also, being able to regain focus quickly is a critical element to achieving a high level of mental toughness.

Jack Bauerle, legendary Olympic swim coach, also spoke about life lessons taught through sports in my interview with him. He believes one of the most important behaviors that separates sports champions from others is their discipline and willingness to give their all, even on their worst days. He elaborated: **"The biggest difference between the very top athletes and others is that they bring it every day. Even if they are having a bad day, they don't let it turn into a terrible day."** He further commented: *"They find a way to get something positive on the days they are physically and/or emotionally spent. Athletes need to muck through the days that are not smooth. Those are the most important days."*

John O'Sullivan, soccer coach and author, has a similar outlook on what it takes to achieve greatness. He believes it is a combination of talent and a willingness to suffer. By suffering, he means working harder than everyone else. It might mean getting up at 5:00 a.m. to train or perhaps outlasting your peers in working on your skills. Thus, he believes the best thing coaches can do is not to coddle their best players, but instead to push them to work harder than everyone else to achieve greatness.

Kurtz ensures he doesn't coddle his top juniors by not letting them cut corners. He commented: *"Extra discipline is needed so they don't cut corners in their training and preparation."* He tells his players there is no shortcut to success, and that they need to give their best effort whether they are in practice or playing at Wimbledon. Discipline, to me, also includes doing the small things (such as dieting, off court training, and resting instead of staying up late) when you don't feel like doing it. That kind of discipline and dedication are required to reach your full potential in tennis.

Outstanding coaches like Kurtz also understand the importance of cultivating a "growth mindset" in their players. According to Carol Dweck's book: "Mindset: The New Psychology of Success," those who have a growth mindset believe it is through hard work and effort, not talent and inborn traits, that we achieve our goals. A growth mindset is the opposite of a fixed mindset whereby inborn traits and talent are believed to be the key to achieving success. Without a growth mindset, players will generally not have a willingness to push themselves to reach their full potential.

Without a growth mindset, aspiring players won't truly buy in that their consistent, hard work is instrumental to reaching their goals in tennis as well as in life. Coaches and parents should be praising the hard work, effort, and dedication. That will help to ensure aspiring players continue to put in their best effort.

The overlying message is that if you are internally or intrinsically motivated, put in the hard work, have the right attitude, stay disciplined, focused, and make sacrifices, the results generally will eventually follow. Coach Jack Bauerle also commented that it's not just talent that makes the difference in an athlete's success. He noted: *"Effort and attitude can make up for a lot of deficiencies."*

Dr. Jim Afremow, sports psychologist, believes attitude is *"a decision and also a learned behavior requiring discipline and energy to sustain."* Further, Rob Rotella, sports psychologist, noted: *"Anyone can have a great attitude when things are going well. Can you have a great attitude when things haven't yet gone well?"*

(This page intentionally left blank.)

What does "winning" mean in the landscape of highly competitive junior tennis and beyond?

Tennis is a wonderful sport in so many respects, however, in speaking to several of the experts and top juniors I interviewed in writing this book, they made it abundantly clear how important it is to be playing for the right reasons. Coach Brett Kurtz perhaps said it best: "*If you don't feel the joy in playing, what is the point?*" He thinks that many aspiring players have lost the joy, which is sad for the players and bad for our sport.

Kurtz believes one of his key responsibilities as a coach is to help his players learn to enjoy and appreciate the process of developing their game. He also understands that having the right attitude is critical to player success now and in the future. His thinking was heavily influenced by Jim Dinkmeyer, a coach and psychologist who ran a training program called ACE (Achieving Consistent Effort). He credits this training program with "*opening me up to how a change in attitude and thought process can enhance one's performance.*"

Kurtz gave the example of Andre Agassi who always had great talent but didn't always bring the best attitude. In Agassi's book, "Open: An Autobiography", he talked about how his dad pushed him into playing tennis from a very young age and how he rebelled by using drugs. Agassi made a realization towards the end of his playing career that he wanted to be the best player in the world and was willing to do whatever it took to get there. It was at that point that he disciplined himself and decided he wasn't going to waste any more of his precious time on the planet to pursue excellence. He was finally playing for the right reason!

Kurtz' enthusiasm for the game is infectious, and he uses this enthusiasm to help his players understand and fully appreciate the opportunity they have to compete, learn and grow (both as players and people). Fundamental to his coaching philosophy is helping players learn to lose their results orientation. Focusing on results, or in other words, looking for or expecting instant gratification, is a huge problem, especially for the younger generation. Kurtz referred to this as *"instant gratification nation."* He noted: "*Focusing on the outcome* (instead of the process one needs to go through to develop and reach one's goals) *is why many people lose in the game of life.*" By being too results oriented, players put too much pressure on themselves to perform and win.

Pete Sampras talked about how he benefitted from having his coach take a long-term approach to his development in his book "A Champion's Mind: Lessons from A Life in Tennis." As a junior, His coach had the foresight to have him switch from a two-handed to a one-handed backhand because he believed it would help his attacking style when he reached the next level. It was a calculated risk, that certainly paid off. Sampras said a biproduct resulting from this was that he learned to be okay with losing, since for the short-term, his results suffered. He also talked about how it benefitted him by taking a lot of pressure off of him because he was not expected to win all the time as a junior. He noted: "*I learned to deal with losing without having my spirit or confidence broken, which would help me immensely over time.*" He also noted that because he didn't fear losing, he never choked throughout his professional tennis career.

Although the pressure to win is sometimes self-imposed, it also often comes externally from parents, teammates, and others. Kurtz drills his philosophy into his students minds by reminding them: *"It doesn't matter what the score is, it's always zero-zero."* He firmly believes that the ability to let go of results is critical to success and happiness in life and on the court.

Kurtz fully understands that he is going against the grain with this philosophy, as most competitive players (and their parents if applicable) want and expect to win now. Nonetheless, he doesn't waver from his philosophy. If the player, and his family or larger team, is not open to taking a longer-term perspective, he'd rather not coach them.

James Clear, author of "Atomic Habits," also supports a philosophy focused on future development. He wrote: *"You should be far more concerned with your current trajectory than with your current results."* In other words, focus more on what you need to consistently do to get to where you want to go, and don't worry so much about today's results.

Part of how Kurtz' philosophy plays out with his students is that he is always thinking toward the future in his coaching approach and outlook. For example, he starts teaching young players mental toughness tools and tactics that they will need to be successful years later. He noted: *"Most coaches work with juniors on technique and ball striking first. I work with rituals from the start with kids"* (note: this is similar to what Dr. Jim Loehr teaches). He also commented: *"You can't start too early to work on your attitude and mental toughness since we spend way more of our time on the court actually not hitting tennis balls."*

Kurtz, like other top coaches, understands that the better his players become, the more pressure they will likely face: more pressure to win, achieve a higher ranking, get a full ride scholarship, etc. To prepare them for this added pressure, he teaches them how to handle themselves in competition by having them practice mental focus skills, coping techniques, and rituals over and over again – things that will help them in the toughest match situations they may face. After all, if they can't keep their composure in competitive situations, they will be more inclined to quit, burnout, or simply not able to play up to their potential.

Kurtz also gives his players performance development goals to work on during matches, even though these goals don't necessarily support winning in the present. An example he cited, is that he will instruct his to players to serve and volley each time they get ahead 30-love. Serving and volleying is generally not a winning strategy for a young junior player without a relatively strong serve, but this performance goal teaches his players to develop skills they will need in the future (3 to 5 years from now) to take their game to the next level. His philosophy is that *"You need to learn to do things during competition, not just in practice."*

After each match, he won't focus on why they won or lost. Instead, he'll focus on how his players did in working on their goals, including applying consistent effort and doing their rituals. He also encourages his players to evaluate their own performance, noting: *"if I've trained them well, they'll generally know when they've done a good job executing their game plan."*

The concept of using performance development goals not only helps players build their game for the future, but it is also a great way to improve their mental toughness. Kurtz believes that choosing to do something that puts you out of your comfort zone when under pressure is a fantastic way to increase your mental toughness.

    One of my regrets, and I also heard this from a couple of players I interviewed, was not being willing to take sufficient risks and try new tactics when in match play. My natural tendency was to play the percentages, which generally meant choosing shots I was comfortable with. I thought that playing it safe was the best way to give myself the best chance to win. I think by taking the conservative, short-term approach I held myself back from fully developing my game under pressure. It's one thing to do it in practice, and another thing to do it when you are playing in a third set tiebreaker!

    I believe being willing to try out new, unproven ways in pressure situations ties in well with the concept of viewing competition as a challenge, not a threat. If you view it as a challenge, you will tend to be more comfortable challenging yourself and not be afraid of the outcome.

    Parents who don't buy in to the long-term development approach are typically too results-oriented ("win now"). Results-oriented parents who push their kids to win today may ask questions like: "Why isn't Johnny moving his feet." The answer is likely because Johnny is too tight, and possibly because he is afraid to lose to an "inferior" opponent. Coaches like Kurtz work with the player and family to help alleviate that stress. He noted: *"You need to eliminate the worry about losing and impressing others, and ultimately the stress will go away."* He believes if you train yourself to give your best effort every day and you have the right attitude and are disciplined, the results/improvement will eventually come.

To Kurtz' credit, his students that I interviewed for this book all seemed to have internalized his philosophy and were quick to point out how it has helped them to enjoy the game more, and to develop into better, more mature, and mentally tougher players.

Parents may also need to learn (or be taught) to rethink how they communicate and react to the wins and losses to help alleviate unnecessary stress. The "bad" tennis parent will tend to get easily frustrated when watching their child play. When their child loses, they can be most supportive after the match by listening and saying very little. For example, they might simply say encouraging things like "I'm sure better days are ahead if you keep working hard like you are doing." A good rule of thumb is to ask your child if he would like your input before offering it. Also, it's helpful to cheer during matches when your child does well and encourage them to give their best effort and have fun.

Amber McGinnis, who earned a full ride tennis scholarship to University of Florida under Kurtz' tutelage, had this to share: *"I can't focus on things like, I have to win this match. That will only put pressure on myself and make me overthink. I've learned to focus on the now, not what's going to happen 5 minutes from now, or what was going on before I arrived for the match."* She added: *"This has helped me to stay more level-headed and calmer and made me a more mentally tough player."*

Michelle Eisenberg, former number one singles player at Binghamton University, also talked about the importance of staying in the present and not looking ahead when she is competing. *"I can get tight and become frustrated when I'm thinking ahead. When I get frustrated it's almost always self-induced and not because of what my opponent is doing. When I get tight in matches it's usually because of some judgment I've made like I am supposed to win, or the other team is weak. My coach has helped me with this. I don't freak out as much when things don't go my way.*"

Kurtz commented: *"You need to be in a comfort zone to grow as a person and as a player. The only thing that's real is how you feel."* Ideally, players should learn to love playing each and every point. He noted: *"if you are not in love with what you are doing, highly competitive tennis can be very hard."*

Like Coach Kurtz, I believe the coach can and should play a key role in developing the whole person, not just the tennis player. Parents can also support this by being long-term orientated and not outcome based. In other words, parents should be taught to recognize that it is a journey and to be patient along the way with the inevitable ups and downs. By having this support from coaches as well as parents, players can learn to understand and appreciate that everything is a process and develop the maturity to not expect instant gratification in tennis or in life.

Another benefit of having coaches and psychologists teach players to play for the right reasons (love of the game and embracing the competition) is that they are far less likely to suffer from excessive nerves and stress during matches. This reduction in stress is a key element in avoiding potential player burn out and/or wanting to quit when things get tough.

(This page intentionally left blank.)

Moving from destructive to productive self-talk

"I start thinking, am I capable of doing this? All the negativity coming at me all at once. That little voice in your head doesn't stop. I blink and it is 5-0. Everything stopped being fun."—Anja Tomljanovic, WTA professional

Being able to avoid getting overly self-critical or become your own worst enemy is a major component to achieving a winning mindset. To avoid destructive self-talk, the first step is to become aware of your thoughts while playing. In general, the more aware you are of your thoughts during matches, the easier it is to avoid becoming overly self-critical and self-defeating.

It is important to understand that our brain is hard wired with a negativity bias and operates under a safety-first principle (source: "The Champion's Mind: How Great Athletes Think, Train and Thrive" by Dr. Jim Afremow). That's why we default to beating ourselves up when things aren't going our way. It's also why it is very common to play small and hold ourselves back from taking sufficient risks that will help us grow and take our game to the next level.

Dr. Jim Afremow, renowned sports psychologist, stated on a podcast that *"the voice in your head either helps you win or gets in your way."* He also noted: *"if you start having negative thoughts it's important to realize you are not failing since it is normal. You should treat it as a reminder that I am not going to go down that path and turn it around."*

In Dr. Afremow's book, he mentions the old Cherokee legend known as the tale of the two wolves. One wolf is positive and beneficial, while the other wolf is negative and destructive. These wolves fight for control over us. The point is that we should monitor what we tell ourselves and always "feed" the good wolf. Understanding that this choice is yours alone is very empowering and important.

Anne Grady, author of "Mind Over Moment: Harness the Power of Resilience" offered an interesting tip to not let your negative voice get the better of you. She suggests you give your negative voice a name (such as Helga or Bud) and simply tell it to shut up or go away when it starts to bring you down. Every time you hear your inner voice telling you things like "I'm not good enough," "how did I screw up" or "what's wrong with me", you simply tell Helga or Bud to shut up, go away and leave you alone. Also, she suggests you remind yourself that these negative thoughts are not the truth.

Whether you can see yourself using the "Helga or Bud" tip or not, it's important to find some way to not allow your negative voice to take control over your thoughts.

If your tendency is to become self-critical (which is true for most players), another way you can flip this is by proactively using positive trigger words and positive body language. As an example, your trigger word can be "yes" when you execute your shots effectively. By telling yourself "yes", it can trigger or remind you of what you are doing well to raise your confidence and to exhibit positive body language, like pumping your fist.

Another approach that can be helpful is to tell yourself "no matter what" I am going to do X, Y and Z, especially when playing big points. For example, before a big point you can say to yourself, "no matter what I'm going to clear the net on every shot", or "no matter what I'm going to attack my opponent's backhand if I get a short ball." When I find myself being defensive, especially on my return of serve, I like to tell myself "commit to hit." These three words help me to loosen up and play more aggressively instead of passively. If you can live up to such self-commitments, it can help you avoid tensing up by focusing on your tactics instead of the outcome (that is, how much you want to win the point or the match) or your negative thoughts.

Former top 100 ATP pro, Jeff Salzenstein, is a very big proponent of self-talk. He suggests players give themselves directives of what to do. He also believes that players should ask themselves questions when they miss shots instead of playing the victim. For example, when you miss a shot, he suggests asking questions like *"what could I do to hit my backhand better"?*

Another recommendation is to always focus on what you want to happen, and not what you don't want to happen. For example, it's never a good idea to think or say to yourself *"Don't double fault"* or *"Don't hit into the net".* It's like telling yourself: *"Don't look at the pink elephant."* Once that thought enters your brain you cannot help to think about the pink elephant! These thoughts actually plant the seed in your brain to make errors and make it more likely you will actually do so. Instead, tell yourself what you want to do. For example, *"Get your first serve in"* or *"Hit the ball deep into the court".*

Coach Larry Willens believes in using simple words or phrases to get yourself to do what it needs to do. He instructs his players to simply say "deeper" when their shots are coming up too short in the court or "wider" when their shots are landing too far away from the sidelines. He also advocates for using a set word or phrase when you fix your strings between points. He said this is a good way to remind yourself to be positive and play your game. The phrase should be individualized so it is meaningful to the player. It could be something as simple as *"Play to win"*. My personal favorite is to say "right here, right now" to get myself focused on the present and get mentally ready for the next point.

It's also important to have faith that when you make mistakes or errors, you will bounce back and play up to your capability. Positive self-talk serves to prevent you from dwelling on your mistakes or bad luck, and instead can lift you up to believe in yourself moving forward. When fear or self-pity makes you want to say something like bad things are about to happen, reverse this, and tell yourself that great things are about to happen.

Lastly, as covered earlier in this book, an important element to maintaining a positive mindset as well as positive self-talk is to remember to give yourself permission to miss. This is an especially powerful concept for players who tend to be perfectionists on the court. By giving yourself permission to miss, it is easier to maintain an even keel and continue to demonstrate positive body language throughout your matches, regardless of how well you are playing. **Always strive for excellence, not perfection, since perfection is not achievable.**

Managing your emotions

"There are a lot of great juniors who have a very high level, but mentally, they are not quite there yet."—Denis Shapovalov

"By its nature, tennis is an emotional game. Of course, it may not look it from the outside, but it is constructed to be a one-on-one, non-contact fistfight."—Dr. Allen Fox

Tennis players who are able to stay composed and poised, especially when things aren't going well, have a considerable edge. Further, mastery over one's emotions is a key component to winning in sports (Source, "The Psychology of a Winner, 2020 Documentary on peak performance and sports psychology" 2020). This documentary covers 5 elements that are key to mastery over one's emotions:

1. **Overcome your frustrations** – we get frustrated when we don't live up to our personal standards and potential. When you can't overcome your frustrations, it turns a positive attitude into a negative one. Takeaway – honor the struggle or challenge that comes with frustration instead of fighting it. Learn to laugh at yourself and accept when you make errors on the court. Your motto can be *"little things affect little people."*

2. **Learn to manage rejection** – for tennis players, rejection might mean not making the college tennis team or not being offered a full-ride college

scholarship. Rejection in a positive sense can fuel us to work harder to achieve our goals. Even the great basketball star, Michael Jordan, was once cut from his high school basketball team!

3. **Overcome complacency** – our comfort zone discourages us from changing and growing and taking chances. *"Comfort is the enemy of achievement."*

4. **Overpower your fear of failure** – remember that failure is an important part of the learning process. We can't succeed without having the courage to take risks and endure failing first. Another way to look at this is that you need to fail and then succeed to learn how to get to the next level.

5. **Leverage pressure** – for winners, pressure leads to increased motivation and a sense of urgency. Learning to cope with stress is an important step. Pressure situations test us and allows us to grow and get stronger.

When you are feeling positive emotions, you tend to feel good about yourself and you generally will play better. Conversely, when you feel frightened and threatened your play will suffer. I think a very common reason we may feel frightened and threatened is that we are worried about the fear of failure. Dr. Allen Fox believes that one of the main attributes that separates champions at the professional level from other pros is their ability to control their emotions, including fear.

Roger Federer, Bjorn Borg, and Chris Evert are examples of great champions who did a good job of not letting their negative emotions impact their performance. These champions have all shown the ability to make themselves feel cool and relaxed no matter what is happening in the match. Jimmy Connors, on the other hand, would pump his fist after a great point to get himself and the crowd going to make him feel good, and help to raise his level of play. Interestingly with Federer, he admitted that it took him about 3 years to "find himself" on the pro tour. Armed with the self-awareness he had gained, he decided he was going to act and behave in a way that gave him the best chance to be successful. Clearly, he had learned that keeping his emotions in check gave him the best chance to win.

Dr. Allen Fox claims that psychological research has shown that by nature our emotions tend to override our logical brain, so it takes high motivation and constant effort for the logical side to win out! Further, under the stress of a highly competitive match, players need to be extraordinarily motivated to prevent their natural, unconscious urge to "escape" (that is, give in to the emotional side of their brain).

Regardless of level of play, competitive tennis players can benefit by learning to acknowledge, anticipate and control negative emotions such as anger, frustration, fear of failure and the urge to quit. By controlling such emotions and the temptation to quit and/or make excuses, they give themselves the edge over opponents who give in to these stressors by losing motivation, making excuses and/or tanking matches. Dr. Fox' golden rule is: "**Don't do anything on the tennis court that doesn't help you win.**" Well stated Dr. Fox.

(This page intentionally left blank.)

What does it mean to be mentally tough?

"I'm not afraid of anyone, but sometimes, I'm afraid of myself. The mental part [of tennis] is very important."— Justine Henin, former world number one and winner of 43 WTA Titles and 7 Grand Slams

There is no single definition for mental toughness. Per Laurie Johnson, Mental Conditioning Coordinator for the New York Yankees, mental toughness is *"the ability to perform at your best in spite of the circumstances."* The more challenging the situation, the more difficult it becomes to perform at your highest level. Paul Goldstein, Stanford University Men's Coach, definition of mental toughness is: *"Being able to manage tension and playing the way you want to play when competition is fierce."*

Jim Golby and Michael Sheard conducted research to investigate athletic mental toughness in their study published in the journal Personality and Individual Differences (2004), "Mental toughness and hardiness at different levels of rugby league." Although rugby is obviously a very different sport from tennis, the basics of mental toughness apply across sports. Most would agree, however, that mental toughness is even more important for individual sports like tennis, golf, and wrestling, since you are out there on your own and can't rely on the team to pick you up when you are struggling.

The aim of the study by Golby and Sheard was to investigate the relationship between mental toughness of rugby players and their level at which they perform.

According to this study, **Mental toughness is the one mental skill most frequently identified as the key contributor to peak sports performance.**

Golby and Sheard found that mentally tough performers distinguish themselves on three interrelated levels: (commitment, challenges, and control).

1. Mentally tough athletes tend to be more committed to their sport. They view potentially difficult situations as opportunities for personal and professional growth, and not as a threat. Mentally tough athletes don't give up on themselves or their sport when faced with problems, pressure, mistakes and competition.

2. Mentally tough athletes view adversity as a challenge and respond positively to pressure in ways which enable them to remain feeling relaxed, calm, and energized. Mentally tough players are more able to cope with highly stressful sporting contests and maintain high levels of competitive performance. They have developed the ability to focus and block out distractions.

3. Mentally tough athletes believe they control their own destiny and remain relatively unaffected by tough competition or adversity. They feel more able to positively influence the outcome of competitions allowing them to view competitions in a less stressful manner. Mentally tough athletes are better able to keep their emotions in control and remain calm under pressure situations. If they momentarily lose their

composure, they are better equipped to quickly regain psychological control.

The big question is how do you develop the commitment, challenge and control aspects of mental toughness? Golby and Sheard recommend these tips for developing your mental toughness:

Tip #1: Examine your attitude about adversity. Challenge those beliefs that hold you back from excelling during critical moments in competition. Debate your fears. Remind yourself that challenges help you grow as an athlete and a person.

Tip #2: Learn to use your emotions to your advantage in competitions while remaining in the present moment. Peak performance is all about focusing in the moment on the task at hand.

Dr. Patrick Cohn, sports psychologist, believes that mentally tough athletes share a number of qualities:

(This page intentionally left blank.)

Mentally tough athletes…

1. Find a way, not an excuse – Mentally tough athletes don't make excuses when things don't go their way. Instead of playing the blame game, they take responsibility for their performance, go back to the drawing board, right the ship and try again.

2. Adapt – Instead of doing things the way they always have, they find new ways of challenging themselves, pushing themselves to the outer limits of their potential. They understand what they did yesterday got them to where they are today…but more is required today to get them to where they want to be tomorrow.

3. Expend their energy on things that benefit performance – Mentally tough athletes focus on the things they can control. They don't dwell on the past or feel sorry for themselves nor do they concern themselves with distractions outside of their direct control. They focus on what they can do in the present moment to overcome the challenges of performance and give them the best opportunity to succeed.

4. See the past as valuable informative lessons and nothing more – Mentally tough athletes learn from their mistakes and the mistakes of others, then they let go of the past and move forward. Mentally tough athletes see the past as mental training for better performance in the future. **Mistakes, errors, and losses don't define mentally tough athletes, these experiences strengthen their resolve**.

5. Take risks – Mentally tough athletes understand that fear of failure prevents fully committing to and achieving excellence in their sport. Mentally tough athletes seek out opportunities to move out of their comfort zone. They meet challenges with enthusiasm instead of dread and anxiety. They refuse to be average and understand they may miss the mark on occasions, but it is worth taking the chance in order to achieve great things.

6. Remain persistent despite failure – mentally tough athletes are resilient in the face of failure. They understand that failure is another step in the journey towards accomplishment. They have the mindset that failure is not final and never quit pursuing their objectives.

7. Pursue excellence, not perfection – Mentally tough athletes have a goal, but their focus is on the steps they need to take to get to that goal, instead of the goal itself. They understand that optimal performance is a marathon, not a sprint. Each step along the way moves them closer toward the ultimate goal. They are not embarrassed by mistakes; they do not try to be perfect; instead, they push themselves to the max and seek daily improvement. They understand they will make mistakes along the way and these mistakes are both necessary and critical turning points in their journey towards excellence.

8. Concern themselves with developing their talents and abilities – they don't try to please others, nor

do they resent the success of other athletes. They focus on themselves, their talents, improving themselves, implementing their game plan and achieving the goals they set for themselves.

Dr. Cohn also points out that talent can be overrated. You can find thousands of talented athletes who never achieve greatness in their sport. As a matter of fact, 75% of all teen athletes drop out of sports – not because of a lack of talent – but because they lose the fun in sports and lack the mental toughness to compete at higher levels. He noted: ***"Talent without mental toughness generally results in average performance… But talent with mental toughness makes good athletes accomplish great things."***

The biggest battle in some cases is not the opponent, but rather a player's own mind. Therefore, the development of mental toughness in tennis is not only a critical element, but perhaps an essential. (Source: "The Most Basic Methods of Mental Toughness in Tennis").

At the very beginning – mental toughness in tennis can and should be taught. Like any new skill, it takes a certain amount of time before a high degree of proficiency can be attained in tennis. Because there will naturally be many mistakes early on, beginners need to be taught how to deal with these errors. This is all part of learning. Developing the right attitude toward making mistakes is the foundation for learning mental toughness in tennis. At higher levels of the game, where players may find themselves in highly competitive situations, emotions may play too much of a part in the process of playing. When it gets tight, players may get so tense that they start rushing and their technique breaks down. Additionally, or alternatively, they may get angry and begin to vent in negative ways, such as throwing tantrums, cursing, and abusing rackets. If these players are taught how to deal with mistakes, these mental meltdowns will become rarer.

A good way of reminding a player to not get too worked up over making mistakes is to repeatedly tell him or her that the last point and the last shot should be left in the past. It is the next point that matters now. This generally helps to get the player in the right frame of mind. When the mind is in the moment, a player will be able to summon his or her best tennis. This brings up the next important thing in developing mental toughness in tennis, which is focus.

Focus is the ability to pay attention to things that matter, things that will bring results while at the same time ignoring or simply accepting and dealing with things that cannot be controlled. Focus is something that a player needs to have before and during a match. Even in a practice session, focus is required. When a player focuses, he or she is aware of what his or her body feels at that moment.

A more obvious aspect of focusing is the ability to block out distractions. Whatever is happening in the stands, on the adjacent courts, outside the tennis facility, or anywhere but the court where a player is playing should be dealt with and ignored. Corollary to this, elements like the position of the sun, heat, wind and rain interruptions should also be taken as something that is "just there," and no complaints should be made about it. These things affect all the players, not just one. Things like these do not make it more or less fair for one player or another.

Dr. Duncan Simpson, sports psychologist, points out that it is not realistic to remain focused throughout a two or three-hour tennis match. It is natural to temporarily become distracted by our internal thoughts and external things going on around us. External distractions may include what is happening on the court next to us, people watching us, court conditions, wind, etc. **The outcome you want is to be able to detect these distractions and then refocus back quickly to the task at hand**.

How well we are able to block out distractions that prevent us from performing to the best of our ability is a way to distinguish how mentally tough we are. Craig Sigl, mental toughness trainer for athletes, likes to use this formula: Performance = Potential – Interference. That seems a bit simplistic to me, but I think you get the idea – if you can maintain your mental focus by avoiding negative interference from your conscious or unconscious mind (and other outside sources of interference), you give yourself the ability to perform your best.

James Clear, author of the book, "Atomic Habits", had this to say about mental toughness: *"It's like a muscle. It needs to be worked to grow and develop. If you haven't pushed yourself in thousands of small ways, of course you'll wilt when things get really difficult. Mental toughness is built through small wins. It's the individual choices that we make on a daily basis that build our 'mental toughness muscle.' We all want mental strength, but you can't think your way to it. It's your physical actions that prove your mental fortitude."*

Jack Bauerle, the legendary University of Georgia and United States Women's Olympic swim coach, believes that consistency in practice is a key element to his athletes' success. Jack commented: *"Don't let your bad days turn into your awful days – this is all mental."* He believes if you are consistently good in practice and competition, that will inevitably lead to some outstanding performances.

A good story about mental toughness came up in my interview with George Bezecny. As a senior on the

University of Georgia's men's tennis team, George had just lost a grueling three and a half-hour singles match in the semifinals of the NCAA Championships and felt completely drained. He woke up at 4:30 the next morning and his body felt *"very weak and terrible"*, and his knee was in a lot of pain. Unfortunately, there was almost no time to recover because his team was playing in the championship match against UCLA at 2:00 p.m.

His coach took him to see a doctor at the hospital around 8:00 a.m. and they gave him emergency treatment with IV fluids as he was badly dehydrated. His knee was also still very sore and swollen.

George had to call on his superior focus and concentration to block out the pain and the significance of the match. There were thousands of fans watching the match at the University of Georgia tennis stadium. George said: *"it took a while for me to get going because I arrived only a few minutes before the match and had very little warmup time."*

He lost the first set in about 20 minutes and could have easily folded. Most players would have. He said: *"To this day, I don't know how I even played that match."* Somehow, he was able to find the tunnel vision despite the noise, excitement and all that was riding on the match. He said all of the training and confidence he had built up over the year helped him to lock-in mentally with a rush of adrenaline.

His knee started slowly loosening up, and he found the strength and mental toughness to stage a comeback and win a tight 3-set match 2-6, 6-4, 6-3, helping his team secure their first ever NCAA championship over a very strong UCLA team.

George firmly believes that for him to reach a high level of mental toughness, *"it was necessary to get beaten up first*" and also have the experience of coming through in difficult situations. He said: "*belief has a lot to do with it… you truly have to have the self-belief you can do it… what you think (and believe) is essentially who you are.*" He added, "*As a competitive tennis player you have to battle your opponent and yourself, and the toughest opponent is yourself.*"

George also reflected back on his junior days when he suffered a "traumatic" and painful loss in the finals of an Orange Bowl match. The Orange Bowl is the biggest junior tournament on the tennis calendar. He said he would never forget the feeling of being up in the match and then "*suddenly the guy starts coming back.*" He noted: "*It took me a long time to get out of a rut after losing that match.*" He added: "*The toughest losses to get over are the ones you want to win bad, and you should win, but things go poorly.*" Painful as that experience was, it likely pushed him to work even harder in practice and ultimately become one of the most mentally tough and accomplished college players in the country.

After his college playing days were over, George said he also learned about mental toughness by practicing with pros like Harold Solomon. He said: "*Solomon's intensity was off the charts. He would never quit and would run down every ball possible.*" He also learned by watching guys like Jim Courier and Tomas Muster. "*Those guys are so intense, and they give you nothing. That's also how I try to play, by making my opponent have to work for everything they get. I make them beat me, especially on the big points.*" George also said he was fortunate to have the opportunity to hit with guys like Jimmy Connors and Kevin Anderson, commenting: "*The common thing you can see is the mentality and focus they are practicing with.*

Those guys are always engaged and think of practice as a match situation."

When I interviewed George, we were in the midst of COVID-19. He believed that the COVID-19 layoff would be a challenge for the pros (and other players) to regain their mental edge after having not competed for many months. It's similar to being out with an injury for a few months and trying to regain what you lost.

George added: *"There's no simple formula for learning to be mentally tough, and you have to continually work on it. Developing self-belief is probably the number one thing."*

It's important to point out that being mentally strong doesn't happen by flipping a switch and saying, "I'm now going to be mentally tough." You have to rehearse and practice the appropriate responses, behaviors and rituals over and over. It also takes discipline to focus on the process and joy of competing and not on the outcome. If you don't focus on the outcome, it doesn't mean you don't care about winning!

George commented on what he thinks are the most relevant attributes of a mentally tough tennis player: *"You need to have self-belief, resiliency and focus to perform well under pressure. You also need to be willing to deal with the physical and emotional pains that come with competitive tennis. There are a lot of highs and lows."*

Further, he suggests that aspiring players who want to develop mental toughness should seek out coaches who have been through it and can communicate what it takes. Ultimately, though, it's on each player to pay attention to what works for him or her. Adding: *"With the right mentality and skill, great things can happen. Without the right mentality you will be very average."*

According to Jim Thompson, "Positive Coaching in a Nutshell", mental toughness is suffering discomfort to accomplish something important to us. Thus, when players suffer defeat or are in a tough spot, coaches should tell them it is an opportunity to develop mental toughness. Their performance will improve as they focus away from failure to working on developing mental toughness.

Dr. Jim Loehr believes the two most fundamental ingredients to mental toughness are:

1. Giving 100% fighting effort

2. Fueling your positive emotions regardless of what happens during competition. In other words, continuing to display positive emotions in spite of adversity.

Which of the following statements is more indicative of who you are as an athlete and tennis player?

When the going gets tough, I get excited… or, when the going gets tough, I feel defeated?

The attitude you adopt and the mindset you choose is a key determining factor as to how well you face adversity as a tennis player. Adversity has many faces, such as:

- Tough losses
- Bad line calls
- Coach biases
- Parental expectations
- Rude spectators
- Missed opportunities (e.g., blown set points)
- Personal obstacles (e.g., injuries or illness)
- Mental mistakes

It's important to note that every athlete has faced adversity in one form or another. If you are to be successful, you need to learn how to rise above adversity. It is your decision whether to quit or to keep competing. Adversity can be a steppingstone to something greater or a learning experience that can be used in future similar situations. Remember, you are capable of rising above adversity, but only if you have the right mindset and use your past adversity to your advantage.

Dr. Patrick Cohn, mental game coach, states that to adapt a winning mindset for adversity, you should:

1. Understand you are capable of handling adversity and its only temporary, not long-term.

2. Use your past adversity as evidence to support that you can overcame what you are facing today and become stronger.

3. Remain confident that your performance will eventually turn for the better. Look for the small signs that your game is recovering.

Jeff Salzenstein describes having a positive mindset as: *"the secret sauce that you can't measure. It enables you to go for the serve when it counts, to compete at a higher level and to find ways to win and be successful. It also allows you to learn and grow instead of getting depressed for a month after losing a big match."*
According to Dr. Jim Afremow, author of "The Champion's Mind", there are four things champions tend

to do differently from a mindset perspective. He refers to these as *"The Four Cs"*:

Competitiveness – they tend to be ultra-competitive and have an attitude of domination and are willing to keep fighting to win until they drop. Michael Jordan is a good example, as he is well known for being super competitive and doesn't stop until he finds a way to win, whether it is basketball, golf, playing cards or anything else. Peter Smith, former USC Coach, talked about how he pushed his players to always compete on and off the tennis court, and that you should enjoy crushing your opponents.

Confidence – Jack Nicholas, the former champion golfer, said that *"Confidence is the single most important factor in golf and probably in life."* Championship level athletes tend to remain optimistic, even in very difficult circumstances. They have a lot of faith in their ability and a very positive self-image.

Concentration – they are able to get hyper-focused. When they do get distracted, they are able to re-focus quickly. Their attitude and focus are on what they need to do on the next play or point.

Commitment – they are typically so motivated to work and improve their game that they need to remember to slow down and pace themselves.

(This page intentionally left blank.)

Mindfulness and peak athletic performance

"The more you can be present on every point, I think that's why you see great champions separate themselves at the end of a set or at the end of a match, because they are the ones that aren't changing in their execution. They are not assigning a value to any one point more than another. It is about what they do point after point."— Andre Agassi

Mindfulness is "the psychological process of purposely bringing one's attention to experiences occurring in the present moment without judgment, which one develops through the practice of meditation and through other training" (source: Wikipedia). Based on this definition, I think it is relatively easy to understand the benefit of learning to practice mindfulness to be able to perform well in difficult, competitive match situations.

In the book, "The Mindful Athlete – Secrets to Pure Performance", George Mumford covers the concept of mindfulness and sports performance in depth. He explains: *"When you connect to that deep place through conscious breathing, you're far less likely to get thrown off by whatever distraction or emotional challenge you are dealing with."* Through conscious breathing or what Mumford calls *"Awareness of Breath,"* concentration and relaxation can coexist.

It goes without saying then that a fundamental first step to mindfulness is learning how to breathe deeply and calmly. By practicing deep breathing and/or meditating on a daily basis, over time it will become easier to maintain a relaxed state in any stressful situation, whether it involves competitive sports or any other life endeavor. That's the true beauty of learning to achieve relaxed concentration: it can benefit you in all areas of your life! Personally, I make it a habit to do a brief meditation shortly before I take the court for my matches as I find it helpful in clearing my head and getting my body in a more tension free state.

Mindfulness meditation involves sitting still, quieting the mind through conscious breathing, and practicing what's called *"bare awareness."* Bare awareness is the simple act of being aware, of noticing the thoughts in your mind or the sensations in your body in the present moment. Mumford wrote: *"When your mind is quiet, you can be what the yogis call "the Watcher." You're in a state when you can just watch what's happening in your head instead of being controlled by it."* When you are able to connect to your Watcher, you are able to make space between stimulus and response, and whatever anxiety or distractions you might feel will dissipate. You'll have better control of your responses to things around you – whether it be your opponent's line calls, people watching you play, noises around you, thoughts of self-doubt in your brain, etc. Mumford noted: *"Tension comes when we get swept up in what's happening around us, notably all the reactive chatter in our minds, in our emotions, and in our bodies that we lose touch with the present moment and disconnect from that quiet place within."*

Mumford likes to use the metaphor of being in the eye of the hurricane, and *"no matter how intense the storm, the calm, blue center is always there for you."* He noted: *"We all have this quiet center within us. When you are being mindful, you are able to create "space" between the stimulus and response."* In other words, you can react to the stimulus (e.g., missed shot, opponent giving bad line call, intense heat) with emotions such as anger, fear, or doubt, or you can respond by taking in what is happening calmly and without judgment.

Holocaust survivor, Viktor Frankl, famously described it this way: *"Between stimulus and response there is a space. In that space is our power to choose our response. In our response lies our growth and our freedom."*

Mumford believes anyone can cultivate mindfulness through ongoing practice and fine-tuning his way of being through diligence, focus and intention. He defines diligence as *the continuous application of enthusiastic, poised energy* (you keep applying the effort regardless of the results). The mindful athlete is also able to remain optimistic because he has trained himself to remain confident despite the inevitable setbacks he faces in the pursuit of excellence.

I believe the concept of diligence ties in well with Winston Churchill's quote: *"Success is being able to go from one failure to another without losing enthusiasm."*

Consider the baseball hitter who fails 7 out of 10 tries but is still considered an all-star. Or perhaps the tennis equivalent might be the server who fails to get his first serve in 50% of the time or the returner who has a 70% "failure" rate on break points but does not let that deter him at the next break point opportunity. In contrast, those who are not "mindful" or present-oriented are more likely to mentally take those "failures" to the next serve or next point. The mindful player, being able to stay present, gives himself a better chance to be successful after experiencing failure after failure.

In the classic book *"The Inner Game of Tennis"*, W. Timothy Gallwey described the two "selves" every person has: "Self 1" - the analytical, ego-driven, anxious self that drives many of our actions and preoccupies our minds."

This is the self that moves continually out of the present moment, latching onto various inner obstacles and tripping up our game. "Self 2" is the intuitive unconscious mind that transcends these obstacles and allows us to feel at one with everything around us." Self 2 lives entirely in the present moment and holds the key to *"conscious flow in life"*.

The key to the inner game involves putting Self 2 into the driver's seat and putting Self 1 in the back seat. *"This is the space where mindfulness helps us transcend the mental chatter and patterns of self-doubt and relinquish control to Self 2."* As is the case with any sport or art, the only way to do this is through regular practice.

Being able to toggle between Self 1 and Self 2 is an invaluable technique when you are in the midst of competition, feeling the heat of pressure bearing down, and you want to calm down and access flow even while simultaneously amping up your performance.

When Gallwey describes the principles of the inner game, he is essentially describing mindfulness, practicing non-judgmental awareness, unlearning bad habits, and learning the art of relaxed concentration. Gallwey believes that this intuitive process doesn't have to be learned; we already know it. All that is needed is to unlearn those habits which interfere with this and just *"let it happen."* To tie back to Peter Smith's thoughts on effective coaching, one of the most important things the coach can do is to *"help the player mentally get out of his own way."*

I'd like to also attempt to demystify what it means to get to and be in the zone. When you are in the zone, it's not that you are able to control your thoughts. Trying to control your thoughts whether positive or negative is impossible. **When you are in zone, what you are able to do is allow your thoughts to come and go**. By allowing your thoughts to come and go, you can stay present and have the potential to play in the zone.

In other words, *"mindfulness helps you to achieve flow readiness or have zone experiences"* according to Mumford. Psychologist, Mihaly Csikszentmihalyi, a leader in the field of positive psychology, describes **flow or being in the Zone**, as the act of *"being completely involved in an activity for its own sake. The ego falls away... Your whole being is involved, and you're using your skills to the utmost." "Flow is your ability to stay in the present moment. The ability to stay present is what fosters the Zone experience."*

To be *"flow ready"*, your thought process must be simplified and concerned only with what is happening now to reach your peak performance. Always stay fully immersed in the moment. Dr. Afremow, sports psychologist, noted: *"Thoughts about the past and future are fog, and thoughts about the present – the here and now – are clear skies. When you are clearly focused on the present task, then you free yourself to thoroughly enjoy the experience."*

If your mind is thinking about the past (i.e., the last point) or worried about the future (i.e., fear of losing a match or ranking points), this will also reduce your joy in playing and competing. **If you are not experiencing joy in the present process, you have essentially eliminated the possibility of having a zone experience.**

Personally, I've had several flow or zone experiences on the tennis court where I felt tension-free, effortless, and completely in tune with what was happening. My anticipation and court movement felt extraordinary. In one tournament in particular, I recall winning in the finals of a USTA event against a highly ranked player and feeling like I couldn't miss a ground stroke all day. My strokes required no thought process. On the rare occasions I missed on that day, I easily shrugged it off and stayed positive, present and focused on the next point.

Mumford noted: "Many athletes have extraordinary strength and skills. The real key to high performance and tapping into flow is the ability to direct and channel these strengths and skills fully in the present moment – and that starts in your mind." The flip side of that equation is also true. No matter how strong or skillful you may be, your mind can impede that talent from being expressed, and it often does so in harmful, insidious ways.

Novak Djokovic is a firm believer in using meditation which is a key to being mindful. He noted: *"It really helps you to stay calm. Today, in this modern world, that is obviously very fast, we are always playing, always out, we have so much information coming from phones, from computers, televisions. We are surrounded by a lot of noise, and meditation is really important in my opinion as it helps me to be present, to have a reset, as a person, as a tennis player, as an athlete."*

Djokovic continued: *"We are always alone on the court, so I think it is a fundamental thing to do. I have been doing it for ten years now, and it has obviously helped me a lot on the court but also outside of it, for a normal life"*. He also commented on the importance of effective breathing: *"There are some techniques of breathing that can really affect positively your mental, emotional, and physical health."*

Of course, the tools of meditation and breathing can benefit players at all levels, not just great champions like Djokovic. All of us have the ability to practice mindfulness and learn to stay in the moment.

In Allon Khakshouri's "Ultimate Guide to Becoming a Mentally Tough Tennis Player", he suggests how you can get started with meditation by following these steps:

- Take a stopwatch or timer and set it for 10 minutes.

- Sit still and just focus on your breathing.

- If you feel you need more support, there are apps like Instant Timer that play music, or Headspace and Calm that guide you.

- To build a lasting habit, a good practice is to meditate at the same time, same place, and following the same existing habit (i.e., after taking your morning shower).

Once you get into the habit of daily meditation, it will be so much easier for you to calm down in moments of pressure, both on and off the court.

Since there are countless books and resources related to meditation, and I am not an expert on the topic, I will not attempt to go into more detail in this book.

(This page intentionally left blank.)

Using proper breathing, visualizations and rituals to gain a competitive edge

Proper breathing

Proper breathing technique is viewed as just as critical to competitive success as ball striking and footwork according to coach Kurtz and several other experts I interviewed for this book. Many parents and players, however, do not see it this way. Juniors also generally don't want to work on breathing technique (that is, breathe in through the nose, and exhale as long as you can) and other relaxation techniques. The same holds true for visualization, as practicing, training and playing the game are generally seen as higher priority things to work on.

Proper breathing can be practiced both on and off the court, and it is very common for players to incorporate taking a deep breath into one's ritual between points. Essentially, players should learn how to inhale deeply and use exhalation (deep stomach breaths) to slow things down. Breathing properly can help your body to relax and it also can slow down your heart rate between points. Players who are able to self-regulate their breathing between points give themselves a considerable edge, especially in tight, physically challenging matches.

Probably the best way to develop effective breathing technique that you can rely on is to practice it daily via mindful meditation. Fifteen to twenty minutes a day is all that is required. As mentioned earlier, there are apps like Instant Timer that play music, or Headspace and Calm that guide you in how to get started.

Visualization

According to Dr. Jim Afremow, sports psychologist, visualization, also known as imagery, involves *"creating a crystal-clear mental image and powerful physical feeling of what you want to accomplish."* This should include the sights, sounds, smells and powerful emotions that accompany the total performance experience. The clarity and controllability of your images will improve with practice.

Dr. Afremow noted: *"The aim during imagery rehearsal is to "see it, feel it, and enjoy it"* For instance, bounce the ball three times, take a deep breath, and see your target and inhale deeply. Then, fully see, feel and enjoy executing your serve. Challenging yourself to do this exercise successfully three times in a row with full focus and positive result is suggested. Imagery can also be used as a mental walk-through to pre-experience flawless performances and expertly handling any adversity that might occur during matches.

Coach Brett Kurtz places a lot of importance on visualization to improve the performance of his top juniors. He has them visualize various situations they are likely to face on the court, so they are well prepared to deal with them in the key moments when under stress. He thinks this is a critical reason why his players don't tank and are able to avoid getting overly upset and frustrated.

Coach Kurtz even has some players visualize entire matches. He commented: *"I have one of my players work on hitting patterns while playing a full match. Each point involves striking at least 6 balls. Having him visualize so extensively makes playing the real match so easy."*

Another common visualization his students practice is to get off to a quick start in their matches. He noted: *"Some of my players are notorious for being slow starters. I have these players visualize slowing down between points during their rituals, so they come prepared to better manage their nerves. The first 3 games of every match, I have them make a conscious decision to slow down. After 3 games, now you are into the fight."*

Visualization may also focus on breathing patterns or perhaps a serve plus one shot (i.e., serve up the tee and then hit behind the person). He may also have his students visualize staying low and exploding in hitting a backhand. A visualization may also involve how the player will react to his/her worst mistake.

An exercise that Kurtz typically uses is to have his players visualize how they will respond when they get a bad line call. So, when it happens, they will be ready. Basically, they mentally rehearse calmly asking for a line judge and not get rattled or upset. *"This helps them to be automatic in match play."* Kurtz clearly understands that when a player is not expecting to be cheated and/or is caught off guard by the situation, he is much more likely to self-destruct or at a minimum, need some time to calm down and be level-headed enough to stay the course and compete to the best of his ability.

Armed with consistent visualization practice, Kurtz' players have the tools to not let their emotions take over when they face difficult, challenging and frustrating situations during matches. They make a conscious decision that they will not get frustrated or upset when something goes wrong. Instead, they will stay calm and poised and move on to the next point. The player ultimately needs to decide *"I'm not going to do that anymore"* to give themselves the best chance to be successful and be able to focus on the next point. The visualization used can be customized to the player's needs and change over time.

The visualization exercises have *"helped a lot"* according to two of his students that I interviewed. Deep breathing is typically one of the first things the player will practice over and over so that it becomes automatic to take a couple of deep breaths when they get angry, stressed and/or frustrated.

Players might even write down on an index card: "cheating happens, deep breath" to reinforce the appropriate behavioral response. According to Dr. Michelle Cleere, psychologist, the beauty of teaching juniors (and others) this type of behavioral response is that it can be applied to any difficult situation they face in life, so they are developing as a person, not just as a tennis player.

Jonathan Fromkin, a highly ranked junior who has been coached by Kurtz for over five years, shared how he has used visualization to improve his on-court performance. *"The night before each match, I spend 10 minutes in bed visualizing moving my best and playing my best. I visualize running for every ball and doing my rituals and focusing, hitting high and heavy strokes."* He added: *"It helps to calm my nerves and gets me more excited to play."* His visualization may include an assignment from Kurtz like coming to the net twice per service game to help instill specific tactics to use.

During the COVID-19 quarantine, Kurtz assigned Fromkin to visualize playing matches out on the grass. He would literally visualize playing three sets every day and then would text a video to his coach as proof that he had completed the assignment.

Larry Willens, San Diego State men's tennis coach, also believes that visualization should be practiced off the court before you bring it on the court. As an example, he'll give a player an exercise to visualize hitting five forehands from their racquet to within 2 feet from the sideline. Willens tells his players that their visualizations need to be perfect. In other words, if they do not hit the ball where they want to, they must start over again. Then, when they practice forehands on the court, he'll stand 2 feet from the baseline corner and tell the player to hit the ball off of his shoe.

Layne Beachley, champion surfer, talked about how she visualized every aspect of her victory before it happened. She visualized what bikini she would wear, the smell of the beach, what hand she would use to raise the trophy, and even the taste of the champagne when she celebrated her victory. Source: The Power of Self-Belief, Layne Beachley. **The great thing about our subconscious mind is it cannot separate what is real and what is imagined, so don't underestimate the power of visualization!**

According to Allon Khakshouri, "The Ultimate Guide to Becoming a Mental Tough Tennis Player": There are four variables that will determine how effective your visualization will be:

1. Frequency: The more often you visualize, the better. Ideally, you want to start visualizing big goals before going to sleep, and if you can, also when you wake up in the morning.

2. Duration: The longer each session, the more effective it will be. Start with 5-minute visualizations at first, aiming to get to sessions that last at least 10-20 minutes.

3. Intensity: The more intense you experience positive emotions of actually achieving your ambitions while visualizing, the more emotional juice you create. By having a clear impression of what success feels like, you will also feel more inspired to work hard and push your limits. For example, picture yourself celebrating with your loved ones, and experiencing the impact that your success will leave on the people around you.

4. Vividness: The more details you see in your visualization, and the clearer those images and pictures are, the better. You want to vividly see, feel, and hear the events that lead you to win a great tournament, or climbing up the rankings—as if they are happening to you now in real-time. You also want to picture yourself overcoming some of the obstacles that you might face throughout this journey.

Rituals

Since tennis is a game of starts and stops, what happened in the previous point is never as important as what will happen in the present point. The starts and stops require that a player should also have a mental rhythm consistent with the rhythm of the match he is playing. This is a challenging aspect of developing mental toughness in tennis, and it is where the importance of rituals comes to play.

Rituals help players regroup and refocus. Rituals and the ability to regroup and refocus on the task at hand

help keep the mind in the present. When all other things are approximately equal between opponents, the player who can focus more, stay in the moment more and calmly accept errors more will generally be the player who goes home with the victory. It will not only be because of his or her serve or forehand, but ultimately, because of being mentally tough.

Jeff Salzenstein believes one of the reasons Rafael Nadal is so mentally tough is that his rituals are on auto pilot and that he can depend on them. Salzenstein commented: *"I didn't develop enough routines and rituals which led to inconsistency for me. I was always searching for my identity – am I more like Nadal or Federer?"*

Coach Kurtz noted: *"The most important thing about rituals is to do something consistently."* I teach them to have a fighter image and look at the strings. Find the center box in the strings. The goal is to have "relaxed intensity" on the court. James Clear, in his book Atomic Habits said: *"The more you ritualize the beginning of a process, the more likely it becomes that you can slip into the state of deep focus that is required to do great things."*

Coach Brett Kurtz keeps the rituals simple and has his players repeat them over and over again to ensure they use them consistently during match play. After each match, he will ask for feedback on whether they used the rituals and worked on the specific performance goals they agreed to. He wants his players to have habits that are so ingrained that they will remember to consistently do them without thinking.

Dr. Jim Loehr teaches his players to remain energetic and positive regardless of the score, and rituals are a key to doing just that. Your opponent can break down when they see that nothing they are doing is getting to you.

"Staying calm and confident can shake my opponents" according to top junior, Amber McGinnis. Amber clearly has been taught you can beat a superior player by never getting rattled, being unfazed by the score, and playing the best tennis you can in each and every moment.

To help his players stay in the present, Coach Kurtz teaches his juniors to not overreact to what just happened on the court. As Amber McGinnis noted, *"I tell myself that one point isn't going to make the whole match. I need to stay calm and composed so I don't lose 3, 4 or 5 points in a row."*

Michelle Eisenberg, a top player at Binghamton University, focuses on her breathing and slowing things down between points. *"I walk slowly and confidently to my towel and use deep breaths. I look at my racket, slowing down, breathing deeply and slowly. I also say positive things to myself and mean it."*

Dr. Duncan Simpson, sports psychologist, recommends tennis players do a check on four areas between points:

1. Physical check – if out of breath, walk to your towel. Check your shoulders to see if they are tight.

2. Technical check – Am I in the right position? Do I have the proper grip strength?

3. Tactical check – Where am I serving or returning? What is my target? What is my point plan?

4. Mental check – Use a positive affirmation, take a relaxation breath, and use a focus queue (i.e., looking at your strings before the point).

Does your confidence and self-belief hold you back from reaching your potential?

"You have to believe in yourself when no one else does."—Serena Williams

Former top 100 ATP player, Jeff Salzenstein, shared a story with me on how he set his expectations too low on what could have been a huge breakthrough opportunity in his young career. He was playing a 2nd round night match at the US Open on Labor Day weekend in 1997 against number 2 seed Michael Chang. Salzenstein knew that the match would potentially be watched by millions of people around the world, and he recalled how he was so nervous before the match that he thought he might actually forget how to hit a tennis ball!

He warmed up four times on the day of the match, and he said his main concern was not to embarrass himself. He expended a lot of energy worrying before the match. He was also concerned about cramping up (he had cramped earlier in the summer, so this was in his head), which further depleted his energy.

His goal going into the match was to *"try to keep it close"*. In spite of his nerves, he came out playing well enough to win a tightly contested first set. The crowd was also clearly behind him, smelling an upset opportunity for a young American player.

You would think his mindset would have changed after winning the first set 6-4. After all, he was certainly a very capable player (his resume included All-American honors on a two-time national champion Stanford team) and had a huge serve. Also, all of the pressure was presumably on Chang, who was "supposed" to win, being a top seed. After he won the first set, Salzenstein said he experienced a mental let down because his focus was not on finishing off his opponent. Since Salzenstein only set the bar at trying to keep the match close, it's not surprising that's exactly what he achieved that day. He went on to lose the next three sets 6-2, 6-3, and 6-4.

When I interviewed Salzenstein, he explained that while he considered himself to be a very mentally tough player, sometimes "Little Jeff" would show up at the most inopportune times, in the biggest matches on the biggest stages. My understanding of what he meant by "Little Jeff," is an ordinary kid out of Colorado who didn't fully believe or buy in that he deserved to be there competing and winning against the top players in the game. He commented: *"Deep down maybe I felt I didn't deserve to win. Sometimes, I couldn't watch my opponent before matches because it would psych me out as I thought they were too good."* Perhaps he was thinking to himself, do I really have what it takes to win against one of the best players in the world?

These types of thought patterns tend to repeat themselves with tennis players (and other athletes) when they don't fully have the confidence and self-belief, they are capable and/or deserving of knocking off a higher ranked opponent. Sometimes what we do is put some of our opponents on a pedestal thinking they are untouchable based on factors such as their ranking, how cleanly they hit their strokes, or previous head-to-head results. In comparison, we mentally feel like we have no chance, or we will have to do something extraordinary to win, when in reality, we may be very capable of winning if we bring our best game and effort.

Salzenstein believes if he had had a strong coach to guide him on what to think, and what to focus on to get him through challenging situations like that day with Chang, his results would have been better in his career. Simply put, he thought didn't have enough trust and self-belief to put the pedal to the metal after winning the first set to come out victorious against Chang.

Salzenstein's junior development was both interesting and turbulent. When he was 12, he was ranked number 1 in the country in the 12 and under age division. He said he went through puberty very late so almost everyone he played for the next few years were significantly bigger and stronger than him. During that time, he saw his ranking plummet. I suspect that some of you reading this book may have your own story of how you felt inadequate or unworthy at one point or another based on some life experience.

When I asked Mark Merklein, former NCAA champion and ATP pro about his self-belief, he noted it was *"one of my weaknesses."* He further commented: *"It was weird. I never truly felt like at the Grand Slams I was comfortable in my own skin. It was my battle. It wears you down. I wish I would have been more focused on putting my best foot forward and not giving a darn about other things. I never thought I could get way up there. It happens a lot with many players. At times it would go away for me, and all was good. Then I would hit a roadblock and disappear. It would have been nice to just play and believe. It came and went."*

Lennie Waite, a professional steeplechaser and psychology PhD, wrote that at the top level of any sport, it is important that athletes truly believe that they can achieve their goals. Any doubt or hesitation will serve as a roadblock. White also pointed out, that even the best athletes in the world can suffer from a lack of self-belief. Not surprisingly, successfully achieving a desired outcome in the past increases one's belief in achieving a desired outcome in the future.

What I found surprising, however, was how common this issue of lack of confidence and self-belief can be for players at or near the top of their sport. In fact, four of the former ATP players I interviewed for this book revealed they have dealt with self-belief issues to one extent or another. You would think that such accomplished, highly ranked players would be more or less immune from issues of self-doubt and self-belief, but this was clearly not the case.

As I mentioned earlier in this book, I had a similar experience—playing football as a kid, and then I saw 90% of the boys physically maturing earlier than I did and I mentally lost my edge and confidence. I felt subpar and insecure and became less confident in my early teen years compared to how I was as a pre-teen. I didn't fully regain my confidence until years later.

Was it my conscious or unconscious mind that caused me to lose confidence on the tennis court? I'm not sure, but it was interesting for me to learn that *"about 95% of all thoughts, emotions and learning occurs in our unconscious mind—that is without our conscious awareness."* Source: Gerald Zaltman, PhD, Harvard Business School. Of course, if you want to change your self-beliefs, the only way to do so is to first become aware of them.

You can try this exercise if self-belief is an issue for you – say, "I am," and then fill in the blank. For example, "I am tired," I'm a victim," "I am lazy," etc. After you become aware of what you are saying, then you can flip it... "I am going to believe in myself," "I am going to get out of my own way," "I am good enough," "I am resilient," "I am strong," etc.

We've also probably have been around those who tell us one way or another that we are not up to par. We need to steer clear of that negativity. Writing self-affirmations instead of what we feel proud about and/or what makes us great can be good reminders to ourselves. We also need to stop the negative self-talk.

In researching the topic of self-confidence, I learned that many athletes (including tennis players) erroneously think their confidence is mostly tied to their emotions or how they feel at a given point in time (source: Dial in and Focus with Dr. Duncan Simpson, sports psychologist, and Cindra Kamphoff podcast).

Dr. Simpson made the point that you don't have to feel good to play well. He noted that you can feel terrible and play great, and conversely, you can feel great and play poorly. He explained that **confidence is more about our belief system, so it shouldn't come and go based on our emotions or a bad outing**.

To build up each athlete's confidence, Dr. Simpson likes to use the analogy of a brick wall for their belief system. The athlete will write down one reason they should be self-confident on each brick on the wall. The reasons given can be things like previous wins, amount of practice they have put in, physical conditioning, mental conditioning and mindfulness training. The goal is to help the athlete develop a strong belief system and ongoing confidence, regardless of fluctuations in their performance.

Dr. Cindra Kamphoff, High Performance Mindset podcast, believes that most athletes dream too small. They often let their limiting beliefs get in the way. She also pointed out: *"As we age, we can lose the ability to dream. Perhaps we hear too often that our dreams are too grandiose and that there is no way we can accomplish them, and we start to believe those messages."*

Dr. Kamphoff further commented: *"When we push ourselves to dream one notch more than we normally would, we grow. Dreaming above your comfort zone requires you to consider all the possibilities and to choose courage over comfort. Remember, you might hear that your dreams are unrealistic, impossible or ill timed. Choose not to listen!"*

Would you be crazy to see a sports psychologist?

Although we've come a long way as a society as far as believing there is no stigma with seeing a psychologist, there is still some "old school" sentiment that doing so is a sign of weakness, or worse, that we may be lacking in some mental capacity!

Getting help from a sports psychologist (or any type of psychologist) doesn't mean you are weak. On the contrary, it is a way to take care of yourself, so you can enhance your performance. If you are having an issue affecting your sleep, relationships, family, academic stress, performance anxiety, etc., it will inevitably impact your ability to give your best on the court.

A number of athletes have bravely stepped forward in recent years to talk about their mental health issues, so there shouldn't be a stigma any longer in seeking out help. The cases of Naomi Osaka, Marty Fish, former ATP pro, and Kevin Love and Ben Simmons, NBA all-stars, are well documented. Top athletes are just like everyone else, and in some respects, college and professional athletes are under more stress since there is nowhere to hide when you are competing at the highest levels.

Clearly, the role of a sports psychologist is not to diagnose whether you have some mental illness or deficiency. Although they may serve multiple roles, perhaps the simplest and most common role is teaching players coping skills for dealing with mental roadblocks and stressful situations, with emphasis in handling stressful, challenging and/or frustrating issues players may deal with during competition. I view mental training as being all about giving yourself an edge, not about "fixing what's wrong with you." I think it is clearly time that more competitive tennis players (and other athletes) look at it that way.

Patrick Mouratoglou, former coach of Serena Williams, is not a fan, however, of having tennis players use psychologists. He's of the belief that psychologists *"make you think too much,"* and *"when you play tennis, the less you think the better it is."* He is clearly in the minority though.

Diego Ayala, former ATP player and current tennis coach, strongly believes he would have benefitted from working with a sports psychologist; however, he said the machismo from his culture got in the way of benefitting from such assistance. He revealed that he spoke to a couple of sports psychologists when he was a young player trying to make in on the ATP tour, but he held back in being fully honest and open because he didn't want to show any signs of weakness. *"Back then I was overly self-critical, and it created a lot of self-doubt. That is what held me back"* He added, you need a *"crazy self-belief"* (to be a top pro) *which I did not have."* He went on: *"In my early years as an 18 to 19-year-old pro, I didn't know what to expect, and I was mentally naïve and immature. It was really cutthroat on the pro tour."* He said in retrospect he would have done things differently if he could go back in time.

Similar to Ayala's sentiments, a review published in May 2019 in the British Journal of Sports Medicine found that stigma is the number one reason athletes don't seek out the mental health help they need (source: "Can Getting Mentally Tough Up Your Game? In All Sports the Answer is Yes," August 19, 2019). The analysis included 52 studies that collectively looked at more than 13,000 professional, Olympic, and collegiate- or university-level athletes across 71 different sports. Other common barriers included low mental health literacy, negative past experiences, busy schedules, and hypermasculinity.

Mark Merklein, former ATP player and current assistant coach at University of Michigan, says he clearly benefitted by having a sports psychologist to talk to during his playing days at the University of Florida. *"I learned a lot working with Dr. Singer, an amazing sports psychologist on campus. He would let me talk things out. I'd meet him for lunch, and I'd talk and then he would point me in the right direction.* He continued: *"He gave me two or three things to keep in mind while I was playing."* The most helpful thing according to Merklein was learning to *"focus on the things you can control right now. You can't control if you are nervous; however, you can control your effort and how you react to what is going on."* Merklein said this piece of advice helped him to *"play freer"* and with *"less stress."* He added: *"Dr. Singer also had me pick up books about other athletes who were struggling, and how they would sometimes lock up, and that it was normal. I learned if you are nervous, it means you care, so that is okay. You can't control everything. I got a lot better at handling stressful situations on the court."*

According to Paul Goldstein, former ATP pro and current head coach of the men's team at Stanford University, he makes it a point to talk to his players about what they can control to help them with their mental toughness (Source: Weechats.com, August 14, 2015). He said: *"I tell my players they can control their breathing at intense moments, like when they are serving for the match. They can also control where they are going to go with their first serve, and they can rely on their instincts after that."*

Of course, one of the things players can't control is whether they will win the match or tournament. Clearly most competitive tennis players don't typically walk away from tournaments holding the winner's trophy. This makes it easy to find weaknesses or things we don't like about ourselves, which can be damaging to our self-esteem and ultimately our self-belief.

The role of the psychologist (or coach) can be to encourage athletes to identify and vocalize their feelings, so the athlete can better understand what's causing the situation to be so challenging. Together, athlete and coach can work on finding a way to cope, which might be practicing a relaxation technique, having conversations with parents or teachers, repeating positive affirmations, or helping the athlete learn how to recognize his or her unique strengths off the court.

The earlier you introduce mental skills to athletes, the better outcomes they can experience later in life. They may feel more able to reach out when they are struggling and get the mental coaching they need even before issues arise, allowing them to better succeed in sport, academics, relationships, health, and all aspects of their lives.

Per coach Brett Kurtz, *"You have to be crazy to not have someone to help you talk things out."* It doesn't necessarily have to be a sports psychologist to help you talk through issues and concerns, though those who hold a doctorate in psychology would theoretically have the highest credentials. An experienced psychologist or coach who has been cross-trained and has a keen understanding of the rigors of competitive sports (especially tennis) should have expertise to assist. Although Kurtz is not a sports psychologist, he does tend to specialize in helping aspiring players of all ages deal with the mental and emotional aspects of competitive tennis. Kurtz is also a firm believer in teaching pre-teen players mental coping skills.

Players who have access to a trained sports psychologist or coach (like Kurtz), clearly have the potential to not only help improve their athletic performance, but also to enhance their enjoyment and outlook on life and sports. To truly give yourself the best chance of winning and playing to your capability, it's certainly something worth exploring, especially if you think you could use help with mental toughness issues, self-confidence, frustration tolerance, focus, etc.

As Deena Kastor, "Let Your Mind Run: A Memoir of Thinking My Way to Victory" noted: *"Our thoughts are mental habits that we've made. Our minds are malleable. It takes a lot of work to reprogram those pathways in the brain, but it is possible and, most of all, worth it."*

The psychologist with the most impressive resume with respect to helping pro tennis players reach their potential is probably Alexis Castorri. She started working with Ivan Lendl way back in 1985 and has worked with some of the top modern-day players including Andy Murray, Kevin Anderson, and Simona Halep.

Castorri's story is interesting. As a tennis fan and psychologist, she recognized that Lendl was *"too stiff"* on the court and believed he could vault his way to number one if he could learn to be more relaxed, flexible and focused. She approached him after a defeat to Stefan Edberg to promise that she could turn him into a world No. 1. Her solution was unorthodox, involving aerobics, "jazzercise" and yoga, but seven months later Lendl beat John McEnroe in the US Open final in what Lendl considers to be his greatest performance and moved to number 1 for the first time.

Castorri, shared some insights on how she views the mental side of tennis: *"If you are playing in the rain against an opponent who has beaten you five times in a* row with an umpire who you think doesn't like you, you can curse the situation, or you can see an opportunity to change things. You have a choice." She added: *"80% of tennis is psychological. Tennis is a mirror of life that brings out your personality on the court. You have to deal with frustration, anger, and motivation."*

Castorri made Lendl face his fears of losing. *"A player has to accept losing before he walks on the court. If he can face that fear before a match, then he can put it behind him and concentrate fully on the match."* She went on, *"Ivan wanted to win the U.S. Open and be No. 1. But I wanted him to let go of that idea for a minute. I wanted him to realize that by being the best player he could be, he was already No. 1, and he didn't need the U.S. Open to prove anything to himself. I wanted Ivan to realize he knew the feeling of victory without a trophy, he knew the thrill and beauty of tennis and he understood why he was playing."*

In his matches with John McEnroe, Castorri believed Lendl had become too involved with John the person, and it would be better psychologically if Ivan believed the opponent didn't exist. *"Ivan needed to look through his opponent and just see the ball. He was just a moving target and Ivan needed to hit to certain points on the court."* Lendl noted: *"I always felt that concentration was a big part of my game. The better I concentrated, the better I played. Alexis helped me to concentrate better."* Lendl was also able to accept that he will have good days and bad days, and he knew in his heart and mind he was on the right track.

In commenting on her work with Andy Murray, Castorri said when she first started working with him, Murray was frustrated by his inability to live up to his own high standards. She noted: *"When I looked at early films of* him playing, he played with such happiness and excitement, so my initial thought was that he needed to bring back the zest. But I believe you start that off the court." She went on: "It's natural that when someone puts their heart and soul into what they're doing, they sometimes forget how much enjoyment they once took from it. Andy has lofty goals, and he is hard on himself. In that situation, you need to remember to love the battle, that's why you are out there."

Castorri noted: *"Both Lendl and Murray lost four Grand Slam finals before making their breakthroughs. These are people who have had multiple tries before they have actually made it. These are people who persevere."* She continued: *"You have to be a mighty personality to have victory stolen from you, or for you to lose it yourself, and then to come back the next year, or two years later, and continue to work your way up the mountain. That takes a special kind of perseverance."* She added: *"The ball doesn't care. Even right after you win a grand slam, you can't ever rest. It's about the intelligent management of passion. Every one of these top people is incredibly competitive and fiery by nature, even if you don't always see that side of them off the court. Either it becomes a destructive force, or you channel it to work for you."*

As for Kevin Anderson, he advocates the value of putting mental work and visualization into practice, telling ESPN: *"My dad, Mike, who coached me when I was growing up, was big into the mental side of sport. He always spoke about believing in yourself more than anything. As I carried on in my career, I paid more attention to that, and working with Alexis (Castorri) has been great. My focus is now on how I can become an even better mental competitor because that is what it really boils down to."* Anderson added: *"It's about being able to *hit the ball really well in the big moments, regardless of who your opponent may be and what is going on out there. I feel I'm constantly getting better in that department, and it'll be a focus of mine going forward."*

In the article entitled "How Anderson transformed from bashful beanpole to ruthless hulk" - (Sidney Morning Herald, July 15. 2018) – Castorri spoke about young players, noting: *"You may be an amazing player, but that's only one fifth of what needs to be there. There's mental discipline, there's the management of expectations, there's being able to travel, and there's handling the pressures that come with success. So, their actual athletic ability is only one dimension."*

Castorri successfully transmitted these lessons and philosophy to both Anderson and Simona Halep, two under-rated players who she helped learn to let their passion flow. Darren Cahill, coach for Simona Halep, who introduced Halep to Castorri, said *"No one has a better insight than Castorri into the mental agonies of losing a bunch of Grand Slam finals."*

Experts' bios

Peter Smith's bio:

Coached USC Men's Tennis Division 1 team to four back-to-back NCAA titles from 2009-2012 and added a fifth title in 2014. He was named 2011 USPTA National College Coach of the Year and is the only men's tennis coach ever to lead four different men's programs to national top-25 rankings. Peter has coached, mentored, and groomed top collegiate players for over 30 years on how to win. He also played professionally for 15 months and competed at the US Open and Wimbledon.

As of this writing, Peter has retired from coaching collegiate tennis and has accepted personal coaching positions with Steve Johnson, a four-time back-to-back NCAA champion under Peter's tutelage, and Sam Querrey, perennial top 5 ranked US player.

Jeff Salzenstein's bio:

Salzenstein grew up in Colorado and was the #1 player in the country at 12 years of age. He reached the quarterfinals at the Under-16 Championships in 1990 and was ranked second in Under-18 boys in the United States in 1992. He attended Stanford University and was named an All-American in tennis two years in a row, reaching the semifinals at the NCAA singles championships in 1995.

His first professional win was in 1996, winning a doubles title with partner Justin Gimelstob. At the French Open doubles event, he and partner Petr Korda made the round of 16.

He was injured for much of 1998 and 1999 and had surgery on his knee and ankle. He finished his degree at Stanford at this time. After recovering from his injuries, Jeff climbed to a career high top 100 ranking after he reached age 30.

After retiring at age 33, Jeff created a successful online (as well as in-person) coaching practice called Tennis Evolution (TennisEvolution.com). His practice includes mindset coaching for parents, juniors, and athletes from a variety of sports.

Mark Merklein's bio:

Mark won 4 doubles titles on the ATP tour, and achieved career-high rankings of No. 35 (doubles) and No. 160 (singles) in the world. He was a quarterfinalist competing for the Bahamas at the 2000 Olympic Games in Sydney, Australia. He also played for the Bahamas' Davis Cup team from 1999 to 2005.

Merklein had a very illustrious amateur career as well. He played for the University of Florida where he was a four-time All-American. After capturing the NCAA doubles title in 1993, he won the NCAA singles title in 1994 and was subsequently named the NCAA's player of the year.

After his playing career, he coached tennis professional James Blake (ranked as high as No. 4 in the world) for two years and was responsible for Blake's complete fitness and nutrition program. He also spent six years as a national coach with the USTA Player Development Center in Boca Raton, Florida, and is currently the assistant coach for the University of Florida men's tennis team.

Diego Ayala's bio:

Born in Argentina, Ayala grew up in southern Florida and competed for the University of Miami in college tennis.

As a young player on the junior circuit, he had a win over Roger Federer at the 1997 Coffee Bowl competition.

Ayala turned professional in 1998 and played most of his top-level tennis in the doubles format, in which he reached as high as 100 in the world. He won a total of three Challenger titles, all in doubles.

Ayala has coached Robby Ginepri and Jelena Jankovic. He also worked with Eugenie Bouchard at the Australian Open where she reached the quarter-finals.

George Bezecny's bio:

George grew up in Fort Lauderdale, Florida, and was coached by James Evert, Chris Evert's dad, as a junior player. He played No. 2 singles for University of Georgia team that won the NCAA championship in 1985. It was the school's first NCAA championship. He played behind Mikael Pernfors, former top ATP pro, at the University of Georgia. He finished his senior year ranked No. 7 in the country, earning All-America honors.

George played on the ATP tour after college up until 1996. He was plagued most of his pro career by injuries.

Jack Bauerle's bio:

He was the long-time men's and women's swimming and diving coach at the University of Georgia and is generally regarded as the top coach in his sport in the country. He served as head coach of the United States Women's Olympic Swim Team and was named NCAA coach of the year five times and SEC coach of the year 12 times.

His University of Georgia women's team had an unprecedented 15 year-run where they finished either first or second in the nation. Jack is also an avid tennis player and he along with 3 other players own the world record for most consecutive hours (125!) of doubles tennis.

Brett Kurtz's bio:

Brett earned a full ride tennis scholarship to Florida Atlantic University. He has been coaching top players in Florida for over 25 years, including pros, Vince Spadea, who had wins over Pete Sampras, Roger Federer and Andre Agassi, and Mark Merklein, NCAA Singles/Doubles Champion, ATP Singles and doubles ranking. Top juniors he has coached include: Lindsay Graff, No. 1 18s Fl. USTA ranking, No. 1 Princeton University, Stephanie Taylor, No. 6 Fl. Girls 16s USTA ranking, Emory University, Amber McGinnis, top 10 ranked junior and University of Florida signee, Daniel Dauber No. 1 Florida Atlantic University, ATP ranked, and his twin brother, Bruce Kurtz, No. 1 FAU singles and doubles and ATP Ranked.

Alexandra Osborne's bio

Alexandra hails from Sidney, Australia. She received a full-ride scholarship to Arizona State University where she earned first-team All-American honors. She won the Pac-12 Doubles Championship with partner, Ebony Panoho, giving her college their first ever conference championship. As a senior, she received the Sun Devil Female Athlete of the Year Award.

Alexandra currently competes on the WTA tour and has a career high world ranking of 589 at the time of writing this book.

Jeff Thomsen's bio

Jeff grew up in Newport Beach, California. He was the number 1 ranked junior college player in California while playing at Golden West College. He then transferred via a scholarship to play at the University of Oregon. He also played briefly on the pro tour in South America. Thomsen served as assistant coach for the University of Miami Women's team before he was hired into his present position as Associate Head Coach for the San Diego State University men's team.

Steve Adamson's bio

Steve received a full ride scholarship to San Diego State, and during his senior year the Aztecs were ranked in the top 20 in the nation. After his college career, he briefly played on the ATP tour and was ranked in the top 700 in doubles.

In 2011, he was awarded the USTA San Diego District Association Pro of the

Year. He has also been a USTA Player Development Coach. In addition to running his own tennis academy, Steve is currently the Tennis Director of the Pacific Beach Tennis Club in San Diego. He has coached a number of top juniors, including Zoe Scandalis, who played collegiately at USC and then on the WTA pro tour.

Larry Willens' bio

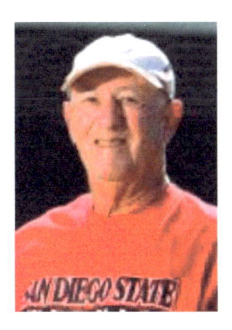

Larry played collegiate tennis for San Jose State and the Naval Academy. He has been a long-time coach at San Diego State, where he currently serves as a volunteer coach. He also coached two professional World Tennis Team squads, the San Diego Friars and Sacramento Capitals.

Larry has worked with some top professional players including Robin White, US Open Women's Doubles Champion in 1988, Gretchen Rush and Kerry Reid. He also coached Rod Laver when he played for the San Diego Friars.

(This page intentionally left blank.)

Experts' winning tips for players

Peter Smith's winning tips for players

1. Get out of your own way! Players can be their own worst critics and hold themselves back. Tennis players are prone to protecting their ego—this is somewhat unique to our sport. You are out there on your own, and to try to figure things out by yourself can be tricky. *"Your mind plays tricks on you."* Takeaway—Thinking too much and being your own worst critic results in lower confidence and poorer performance. Note: Players may need help from coaches or psychologists to get out of their own way.

2. An important first step for any competitive player is to accept the fact that tennis is an imperfect sport. No one plays a perfect match. Even the top pros miss and make errors. Takeaway—give yourself the freedom to make errors. Have patience with yourself.

3. Four to six points in each match can separate players at the collegiate level. It can be as few as one or two points at the pro level. Takeaway—understand that the margin between winning and losing matches tends to become smaller the better you get. Also, how you handle the big points becomes that much more critical in highly competitive matches.

4. To be successful, you should want to crush your opponents. Need to develop that killer instinct. You shouldn't have any care for your opponents. Another benefit to crushing the competition—it can save you energy for upcoming matches.

5. Make sure you have the basics covered to maximize your performance—need to be fit, have a complete game, and have weapons.

6. Learn to be okay with losing. Reflect on what you could have done better, but always look forward and turn the page after each loss.

7. Juniors should play other sports beside tennis while growing up. *"Learning to compete is critical to your success."*

Jeff Salzenstein's winning tips for players

1. Be curious—ask questions when you are not clear and/or think there may be another way to improve your game. Don't simply rely on your coach for your learning and development. Watch tennis videos, read books, etc.

2. Rehearse, practice, and use your rituals and routines to help you stay relaxed and focused

during matches. Practice them over and over so you are on autopilot in match play.

3. Use simple trigger words like "up" to remind yourself to go up on your serve, or "hold" to remind yourself to finish on your groundstrokes.

4. Have a clear strategy, plan, and options for how you will play your matches. That will help to decrease your anxiety. *"If you understand your strategy, you will be more successful and mentally stronger."*

5. If you tend to get tight on big points, tell yourself to "swing for the fence". Your body won't let you over hit when you are tight. If you have the correct technique, your shot will naturally come back down into the court.

6. Instead of being self-critical when you make errors, ask yourself questions (e.g., "What could I do to hit my backhand better?"). Don't be a victim!

7. 80% of our thoughts are negative. We run the same program in our unconscious mind every day. Jeff believes you can retrain your unconscious mind by becoming more aware of your language and how you communicate and choosing to use the right words and visual cues.

8. Become more aware of your hand tension. Aim to be "softer" with your hand and try to be smooth instead of squeezing the racket too hard. "Be like an artist painting."

9. Visualize your targets—visualize the ball arching where you want it to go. Try *"thinking in pictures instead of words."*

10. Visualize, practice, and rehearse your patterns of play (serve wide and hit to the open court, chip your return, and attack the net, etc.). Practice your patterns of play over and over again to get yourself ready for matches. *"Too many players don't practice the patterns and shots every day that they need to break through. You need to be able to hit these patterns in your sleep. Most players just warm up and then play. A lot of times it is just one or two shots that make the difference between a top 75 player and a top 20 player."*

11. Play more matches to improve your mental toughness.

12. Choose an alter ego! It could be Roger Federer, Serena Williams or even Superman. Tap into that alter ego when you play your matches.

Mark Merklein's winning tips for players

1. Your work ethic and discipline are key to your development as a player.

2. Ultimately, it's up to the player to take responsibility for developing and improving his game. Put in the extra time on your own so you are fully comfortable with your game. That will help you to have greater trust and belief in yourself that you are fully prepared to give it your best.

3. It's important that you love to play the game. If you love the sport, you will tend to be more successful.

4. Juniors should play other sports while growing up. An intense focus on one sport at an early age can lead to injuries, and less enjoyment of the sport.

5. Focus on things you can control – you can only control your effort and how you respond to what is going on.

6. It's normal and natural to be nervous in match play. Being nervous is okay. It means you care.

7. To give yourself the best chance to win, stay the course, keep your composure and don't blow up!

8. Be aware and be flexible during your matches – pay attention to what is working for you and your opponent, so you can make adjustments, and pick on your opponent's weaknesses.

9. Don't expect to play as well in matches as you do in practice. It is normal to struggle in matches. Strive to get to 70% and be okay with that.

10. Be your own best coach – feed yourself positive thoughts. Be patient with yourself early in matches, as it may take some time for you to raise your level of play.

Diego Ayala's winning tips for players

1. Have a routine before you step foot on the court – doing the same things over and over gets you mentally prepared and more relaxed.

2. Don't allow yourself to get too high or too low. The best pros are able to lock in on the very next point after a high or a low point in the match.

3. Focus on what you can control—remove the outside distractions and simplify your game plan.

4. Don't be like the crowd and expect instant gratification. Put in the time and effort to develop different aspects of your game. The results will come from your body of work.

5. It's okay to fail—make as many mistakes as it takes to do something right.

6. Learn to be self-sufficient – take the initiative to get better and hold yourself accountable for improving. Don't depend on others (e.g., coaches, parents, etc.)

7. Don't worry about tomorrow. Focus on "winning the day" to be fully present. If you have a bad day, trust that tomorrow will be better.

8. Incorporate your other interests and passions into your training—cross-training for juniors in particular can be very helpful in developing the athlete and avoiding burnout.

George Bezecny's winning tips for players

1. Practice with a high intensity level, both mentally and physically, to prepare yourself to perform well in matches. Always be engaged in practice and think of it as a match situation.

2. Focus on what you can control. You can't control what your opponent does.

3. Get in top shape so you can maintain your energy level and focus both in practice and in matches.

4. Your toughest opponent is yourself. Work on keeping yourself in a positive zone. It is much easier to be negative than positive.

5. Be willing to endure getting "beaten up" and losing. It is part of the learning process to develop your mental toughness.

6. Don't get ahead of yourself in matches thinking about what's going to happen. Stay in the moment, even if the moment is difficult and traumatic!

7. Remember to breathe deeply. It will help you to slow down your body and your mind.

8. Show your opponent that you won't beat yourself. Make your opponent earn the points, especially the big points.

9. With the right mentality and skill, great things can happen. Without the right mentality, you will be only average.

10. Ultimately, it's on the player to push himself and perform. Take responsibility for improving your game, mentality, and focus.

11. Great players are not born mentally tough. Even the top pros have to continue to work on it.

Bruce Kurtz's winning tips for players

1. Take a long-term approach to developing your game. Set performance goals to make yourself a better player down the road.

2. Don't focus on results. Instead, focus on giving your best effort every day.

3. A strong mind leads to a strong body (not the other way around).

4. Take responsibility and accountability for your own behavior.

5. Embrace and enjoy the process of developing your game and the challenge of competition. His motto: *"If you don't feel the joy, what is the point?"*

6. It is more important to have the will to prepare to win (i.e., disciplined training) than it is to have the will to win.

7. Slow yourself down via deep breathing and learning to use rituals.

8. Eliminate excuses.

Alexandra Osborne's winning tips for players

1. Review your game plan the night before your match like you are preparing for an exam. Visualize point situations and anxious situations you may face so you have "lived them" already.

2. Slow down between points to avoid rushing. Think about how you want to play the next point to facilitate being the aggressor.

3. Write down notes after each match when you lose and discuss with your coach. Then, let it go.

4. Play the ball, not the person. *"Who cares if your opponent is higher ranked, lower ranked or your friend!"*

5. Train smarter, not harder. Too much time on the court can lead to injuries. Training mentally (off the court) is also very valuable to your development.

6. Give yourself a break by not being hard on yourself when you don't play up to your expectations – especially if you are a perfectionist. You can't be on 100% of the time.

7. Strive to be a well-rounded person so your whole identity isn't tied up in your sport.

Jeff Thomsen's winning tips for players

1. Use positive self-talk to set yourself up for success.

2. Attitude goes a long way on the tennis court. Even if you are not playing well or down a set, exhibit positive body language.

3. Focus on your breathing on a regular basis on and off the court. Jeff is also a strong proponent of practicing yoga to reduce tension in competitive tennis.

4. Take pride in what you are doing. Play for your teammates, your family, etc., not just for yourself. This will help you to be motivated and fight harder on the court.

5. Your mind is your best weapon as a tennis player. Take the time to invest in your mental skills.

6. Embrace the pressure – don't shy away from it. You should want to be playing in pressure situations. The more it counts, the better.

Steve Adamson's winning tips for players

1. Don't overthink it. Trust the work you have put in has prepared you to play your best. Let your body's muscle memory do the work.

2. Don't be afraid to lose. Have the courage to play your game during the biggest moments in the match.

3. Raise your intensity and focus on the big points.

4. Positive thoughts and positive energy are critical. Remind yourself that you are good, especially when you are down.

5. Maintain your composure and confidence even after you lose a few points in a row. Slow down and continue to compete mentally and physically for every point.

6. Train the mental side of your game the same way you work on your technique.

Larry Willens' winning tips for players

1. Take a few extra seconds before playing each big point to be in control of yourself and tell yourself where you will hit the ball in the next point.

2. If you get a bad line call, tell yourself to go get the next point. If it happens again don't aim your shots so close to the line.

3. Learn to play for yourself. Do the best you can to win each point for yourself.

4. Focus on being the best you can be in practice. Pretend each point you play in practice drills are real points and focus to win each one.

5. Get more depth on your shots by getting more net clearance.

6. Visualize what it looks like and how it feels to hit your shots two to three feet from the sideline. Strive for perfection when you visualize.

7. Believing in yourself is the most important thing. This comes from relaxation, focus, and visualization.

Experts' winning tips for coaches

Peter Smith's winning tips for coaches

1. Help each player figure out how their game can win. Keep the game plan and tactics very simple – it should be something that each player is comfortable with. Note: sometimes Peter will ask his players what is and is not working for them during or after matches to help gauge their level of self-awareness. Takeaway—coaches should help players understand their strengths and how to utilize them most effectively in match play. Related point: one's personality plays a key role in the style of play each player will be comfortable with. For example, if the player is not a risk taker, don't push them to play an attacking serve and volley style.

2. Teach players to accept that it's okay to make errors. Don't dwell on their mistakes or faults. Focus more on what they are doing right. Avoid getting down on players who are underperforming.

3. Building people up is important in raising players' self-confidence. *"A compliment (positive feedback) goes a lot further than a criticism."* Players benefit from coaches that build up their self-esteem and help them mentally get out of their own way. Young players with higher self-confidence also tend to try harder and not quit when the going gets tough. To help raise the self-confidence of his

players, Peter would sometimes write notes to his players the night before a match. For example: *"You're the toughest player at this tournament, and you'll show it again tomorrow."*

4. Demonstrate patience when coaching and teaching. Resist the temptation to jump in and try to correct the player. Often it is better to wait for the player to figure things out, and then recognize and emphasize what they are doing right.

5. Managing the player/parent/coach relationship is challenging, but important to your success. There is a lot more "noise" in kids' brains today than there used to be. The best coach/player relationships often involve parents who are more or less willing to leave the coaching to the coach.

6. Key goal of any coach is to gain the trust of his/her players and team. Further, Peter believes that coaches should be invested in the personal development and well-being of their players, and he was willing to take the time to genuinely get to know his players and then shape and guide their development via one-on-one conversations. He noted *"I care about each player as a person."* Takeaway—the best coaches develop positive, supportive, trusting relationships with players that go beyond the confines of tennis.

7. Instill the importance of competing. "True competitors want to compete more than they want to win." *"So many players run away from the competition when things get tough."* Peter helped

to instill competitiveness in his players by having his teams compete on and off the court. For many players, tennis is their only sport, so he had them compete in ultimate Frisbee, soccer, and other sports. He even had them compete by running up sand dunes together and set the example by running and competing along with them.

8. The coach should help set the tone for players to look forward to competition instead of fearing it or getting anxious about it. Peter's mantra to his USC teams: *"Our matches are a celebration for all the hard work we put in."*

9. The coach should help the team and players to keep tennis in perspective. He quoted Mack Brown, the college football coach, *"Don't make this the most important day of your life."* Takeaway—by learning to keep things in perspective, players will be more well-rounded and perform better in tennis and in life.

10. Teach players to be okay with losing. Although players should reflect on and learn from each loss, they should quickly turn the page and look forward to the next match. Peter's motto: *"There is always another game and another match."*

11. Introduce meditation to your players/teams as a tool to help them learn how to relax and be more mentally focused. Peter is also a proponent of having his players use visualization to mentally prepare for matches.

Jeff Salzenstein's winning tips for coaches

1. Help each player develop and define a clear story of how they see themselves as a tennis player. Help them see a different perspective and to bring their story to life.

2. Help each player to understand the patterns of play that work best for his game. Have players practice these patterns or sequences over and over.

3. Teach and encourage players to model their strokes after other great players strokes. Note: Jeff modeled his serve after Goran Ivanisevic during his time on the Stanford tennis team and this helped to take his game to a whole new level!

4. Customize your approach to the player you are working with. Be flexible with your approach. Listen, learn, and ask good open-ended questions.

5. While you are teaching technique to players, weave in the mental skills that will help them be successful in match play.

6. Work with parents to reinforce positive communication and role modeling. Avoid trigger words like never and always when communicating with your player. Ask questions like: *"What could you do to get a higher percentage of first serves in"*, instead of saying *"You need to get your first serve in more."*

Salzenstein also shared his thoughts on the importance of having a great coach: *"Without a great coach who can see your blind spots, it's going to be very difficult to break through. You are going to lose just about every week, so you need a cheerleader to pump you up. If I had a great coach who worked with me every day on all the shots I was missing in matches, I think I would have had a better career."*

Mark Merklein's winning tips for coaches

1. Take time to get to know to your players – listen to them and gain an understanding of their unique issues, including how they feel about themselves and their game.

2. Relieve the pressure and the stress on players to win. Tell them over and over it's okay to lose and to be nervous, as long as they give their best effort. *"You can only control your effort."*

3. Work on one thing at a time to not overwhelm your players. Keep it simple so they can see the results.

4. Help them to appreciate their ability and the opportunity they have to compete. Help them to see the big picture and keep things in perspective.

5. Give them "tools" to help them relax and stay focused on the court. Have them write out how they will handle certain situations (for example, double faulting at 5 all or on break points).

6. Empower your players to be more self-reliant in improving their mental and physical skills and abilities. Encourage them to read tennis books, watch videos, and listen to podcasts, etc.

7. Be willing to mix things up – taking days off from tennis may be needed to help your player clear his head and recharge. Incorporate cross-training and/or other interests as needed.

Diego Ayala's winning tips for coaches

1. Encourage your players to be self-reliant—raise their awareness about books, videos and other resources they can use to learn on their own.

2. The hardest part of coaching is gaining the trust of your players—work to gain their trust by showing them that you care about them as a person on and off the court.

3. Customize the training and approach you take for each player by incorporating their outside interests/passions—encourage cross-training, especially for juniors.

4. Tell you players that it's okay to fail—you learn and grow from your mistakes. Don't put too much pressure on your players.

5. Stay clear of working with junior and other players who have too much noise from their parents, prior

coaches, etc. Find out early if they are receptive to your input. If not, move on.

6. Don't assume everyone is like you and is motivated to become a pro.

Jack Bauerle's winning tips for coaches

1. In order to trust you, your athletes need to know about you as a person and that you care about them. When they know you care about them, you can be hard on them when necessary.

2. Your conversations need to be customized to each athlete. What motivates one, may not motivate another.

3. Demand punctuality, consistency, and accountability. Punctuality means respect for coaches and teammates.

4. Emphasize effort and the right attitude. These attributes make up for a lot of deficiencies!

5. The biggest difference between the very top performers and everyone else is that the top performers bring it every day! When you are having a bad day (you are physically or mentally tired), don't let it turn into a terrible day. Encourage your athletes to fight through their toughest days and have the discipline to make something positive out of them. In pressure times, the athlete will know deep inside *"I've done everything I possibly could to prepare for success."*

6. Teach your athletes to be "selfish" if you want to be great. The choices you make on your off days are as just as important as what you do in practice. Sometimes you have to sacrifice and not join the crowd. *"The things you need to give up will be a distant memory in 20 years."*

7. Confidence is the X factor. It separates All-Americans from Olympic champions. Pushing your players to work hard and sacrifice will help them to gain confidence over time.

8. On competition days, coach less than more. Keep it simple—you don't want to give them too much to think about. Also, be careful not to pass your insecurities on to the athletes. He cited how 2 of the all-time greatest coaches in college basketball, John Wooden and Dean Smith, rarely got off the bench during games.

9. Teach your athletes to be more self-reliant. *"There is too much stuff being done for young athletes." "They need to muck it up more on their own."*

10. Find ways to make your practices fun. Kid and joke around with the athletes. Give them nicknames to make them feel special and unique.

11. Tell your players that if they want to have a great career, they'll need to endure some great disappointments along the way. Prepare them for the ups and downs of competition.

Brett Kurtz's winning tips for coaches

1. Teach young players to develop as human beings via *"life lessons through sports." "You are coaching a person, not a tennis player."*

2. Teach players to let go of results. His mantra: *"The score is always zero-zero."*

3. Develop the right heart (positive attitude and consistent effort) and mindset (mental skills). Hold players accountable for having a positive attitude and giving consistent effort.

4. Teach players to develop mental skills from a young age. Have them work on visualizations, simulations, and rituals on and off the court.

5. Avoid judging players. Teach them to be self-reliant in evaluating their own behavior and performance.

6. Give players "performance development goals"—aspects of their game they can work on developing in matches to improve for the future.

7. Educate the parents so they can best support the player and reduce the stress to perform/win.

Jeff Thomsen's winning tips for coaches

1. Repetition is critical to developing a winning foundation.

2. Push your players to the limit to make them physically tougher. Challenge them on and off the court (such as, on the track). If they are physically tougher, they will be mentally tougher.

3. Tell your players it's okay to have a little bit of self-doubt. It's only human.

4. Teach your players to embrace the challenge and pressure that comes with high-level tennis. They should relish the opportunity to compete in matches that matter. As Billie Jean King espouses: *"Pressure is a privilege."*

5. Devote time to working on the mental side of the game. *"I tell my players that their mind is their best weapon."*

Steve Adamson's winning tips for coaches

1. Ask a lot of questions instead of telling the players why you are working on specific drills. Have them come up with the answers and why.

2. Make a personal connection with each player.

3. Understand where each player is coming from. Find different ways to approach your players so they are engaged and can reach their potential.

4. Emphasize the importance of staying positive even with the losses. Use a lot of positive feedback.

5. Teach players how to be problem solvers.

Larry Willens' winning tips for coaches

1. Get to know each player well. This is critical to coaching them to be mentally tougher.

2. Give significantly more positive feedback than corrective or negative feedback.

3. Set up score situations in practice (e.g., match point or break point) and play a lot of them. Have it become a habit to play to win so players will not fear these situations.

4. Convince each player to play for themselves, not for their parents, their team, etc.

5. Train your players to talk in a positive way. *"I am going to win the point, not get my opponent to lose the point."* Play to win, not to avoid losing.

6. Teach players to use self-talk in practice so it translates to their matches. If they hit the ball too short, have them say "deeper." If they hit their shots too far from the sideline, have them say "wider".

Player and coach interview highlights

Player interview highlights

I conducted over 20 interviews which focused primarily on mental mindset and tactics. The interviewees included highly ranked juniors, former college tennis players, former pro players, and one player currently competing on the pro tour. Below, is a summary of their responses, including direct quotes.

1. What do you do to try to get yourself relaxed and ready to compete to the best of your ability before stepping foot on the court?

Several players talked about the importance of having a game plan going in to the match: *"The night before each match, I go over my game plan, usually with my coach. It's like preparing to take an exam, so I don't have to rush the day of the match. I have a game plan and visualize the patterns I want to hit."*

A number of other players talked specifically about the importance of using visualization: *"I visualize moving my best and playing my best."* *"I use visualization the night before, playing out point situations and score situations. When visualizing, I'll focus on my breathing and anxious situations I may face on the court, so it's like I've been there before it happens."*

Some players mentioned they like to listen to music to help them be in a good mood and relaxed and/or pumped up before taking the court. *"I want to be clear-headed before I play, and music helps."*

Not surprisingly, some talked about the importance of getting a good warm up leading up to the match. *"I focus on getting my feet moving and seeing the ball clearly."* Two players indicated they liked playing warm up games with a teammate for fun and laughs to help them feel more relaxed.

A few respondents talked about having a routine and sticking to it, so they felt prepared and comfortable. This might include doing an equipment check to ensure they had everything they might need in their tennis bag. Their routines also helped them to be properly hydrated and allowed time to digest their pre-match meal. On the other hand, one player felt it was unhelpful to rely too much on following the same routine or superstitions before each match. She commented: *"I don't want to be thrown off just because I can't eat the same food."*

Three interviewees emphasized the importance of getting in the right pre-match mindset. They used self-talk, and their examples included *"embracing the challenge,"* *"giving my best effort"* and *"don't worry about today's results."* One person said they tell themselves not to think too much, and *"trust that I have put in the work to be well prepared."*

Others talked about arriving early for their matches and allowing adequate time to be by themselves to get centered and calm. Former University of Georgia star, George Bezecny, commented: *"Immediately before the match I get some space and have a frame of mind of not worrying, focusing on taking care of my own game and what I can control. I can't be too high or too low to get in the right zone."*

A few talked about the importance of deep, slow breathing, and one person said that yoga has been very helpful in teaching him how to breathe better and be less tense in tournament play.

2. What do you try to do achieve the right combination of relaxation and aggressiveness during matches to play your best?

The most popular response was to do rituals between points and change overs. Rituals included slow, deep breathing, walking slowly, looking at and/or adjusting strings, and maintaining a strong, positive posture. *"I rush sometimes, so I bring myself back with breathing and taking my time, fixing my strings while I focus on the next point and move past the last point quickly."* One person commented: *"I slow down and take deep breaths, especially after I lose a few points in a row."*

Focusing on a game plan was mentioned as another way to alleviate nerves. *"I like to have some sort of strategy and game plan to focus on." "Having a pattern to focus on helps me to keep my nerves in check." "If you understand your strategy, you can be more successful and stronger mentally." "I like to plan out where I want to hit the next ball to be the aggressor."*

A number of players admitted that one of their weaknesses was having difficulty controlling their nerves the first few games of the match. *"I come out super nervous. Typically, it takes me a few games to settle into a normal anxiety level."* Another player shared: *"I start out more on defense, and not as* aggressive at the beginning of my matches as I should be. *"Usually once I find a weakness or pattern, I can be more aggressive and move the ball around better."*

A few interviewees talked about using self-talk to stay positive and relaxed. *"I tell myself that I can't control everything. This helps me to be more relaxed." "I try to keep myself in a positive zone. Self-belief has a lot to do with it. The toughest opponent is yourself."

A couple of interviewees talked about the importance of maintaining the right energy level. *"I try to be energetic the entire match, regardless of the score."* "*I take a temperature check, and I either pump myself up or calm down as needed during the match."* One person added: "*As I've gotten older, I slow down and spend more time between points* (e.g., going to the towel), *so I can exert more during the points."*

3. What are the most common reasons you lose your cool and/or become frustrated in match play?

The number one answer cited was a lack of execution. Some of the comments included: *"Missing my serve," "double faulting," "hitting it into the net," "I shouldn't be making these mistakes,"* and *"I'm making a bunch of unforced errors."* A related comment from a couple of interviewees was *"I can't execute my game plan."*

The second most popular answer, which I consider to be an offshoot of the top response, was something to the effect of *"Getting frustrated for me is self-induced."* This included negative self-talk and comments like: *"I am my own worst enemy"* and *"The other player doesn't affect me —I don't let them."*

Three interviewees talked about getting frustrated because they were thinking ahead and not staying in the moment. *"Usually, I become frustrated when I think ahead —I get tight because I am thinking about winning or losing the match."* One player commented: *"Staying in the moment is the key even if things are going bad for me."*

A few interviewees said external stuff causes them to lose their cool. Examples cited included: *"My opponent is cheating,"* and *"My opponent is using head games."* One person said they tended to lose their cool when people who are watching the match root against them or heckle them.

Another response that came up a few times was that they were more likely to lose their temper in *"high profile"* or *"important"* matches. In other words, they were more likely to lose their cool when the stakes were higher. This makes sense, since we are typically more on edge when playing a big match, so it takes less to set us off.

A couple of interviewees said that *"losing to someone I shouldn't be losing to"* caused frustration. Lastly, one player commented that *"missed opportunities"* was a key contributor to becoming frustrated.

4. Are you generally able to avoid "overthinking" and being self-critical during matches? If so, how are you able to keep your mind quiet?

The most popular answer for keeping your mind quiet was using rituals such as *"walking slowly to my towel,"* *"looking at my strings"* and doing *"deep breathing to slow everything down"* between points.

The next popular response had to do with making a conscious decision to be self-disciplined. This included comments like: *"I make a choice to remain calm to give myself the best chance to win,"* *"I tell myself I need to stay calm and not blow up,"* and *"I don't want to show my frustration to my opponent."* One interviewee shared: *"I don't overreact to one single point or what just happened. I focus on the next point as soon as possible, and I'm pretty good at bringing myself back."*

A couple of interviewees talked about trying to keep things in perspective: *"I tend to be overly self-critical, so I remind myself to enjoy the competition."* One person said: *"I tell myself it is just a game."*

A couple of respondents talked about using positive self-talk, for example: *"I try to pump myself up by telling myself positive things and I mean it!"*

One interviewee said that he gets too caught up in stroke mechanics, commenting: *"It's hard not to do, even though I understand the less I do it the better."*

One respondent talked about letting self-doubt creep in, commenting: *"I may psych myself out thinking the other guy is too good."* Another said: *"I remind myself that I am good, especially when I am struggling."*

5. What are the most common reasons you lose (other than your opponent was a better player)?

The most popular response had to do with *"getting ahead of myself."* In other words, they felt the match was already won and didn't keep their foot on the gas pedal, or they were too focused on the match results (i.e., winning or losing) to play their best tennis. A related response was overthinking things – *"I felt I needed to win for my team which put more pressure on me."*

The next most popular answer was some form of *"beating myself up."* For example: *"I wasn't happy with how I was playing so I got frustrated and mad at myself."* Another person commented: *"When I was younger, I didn't always have the best attitude. I've learned the importance of maintaining a positive attitude regardless of the score or situation."*

A couple of respondents talked about lack of sufficient energy/stamina and/or being worried about cramping up in the heat.

Two respondents talked about losing focus. One said: *"I was too distracted by my off the court problems to concentrate well."* The other commented: *"I let a bunch of points get away because I lost focus, got frustrated and stopped competing."*

Other responses included: *"I got tight, especially on big points—I couldn't play my normal aggressive style"* and *"My strategy wasn't working, and I couldn't figure out what to do."*

6. What strategies do you tend to use to bring down your opponent's effectiveness and/or confidence?

The top answer was to do your best to stay calm and look confident regardless of what your opponent does. A similar response was to never quit on any point – *"I show my opponent that he will have to earn everything he gets."*

Another popular response was to pay attention to what your opponent doesn't like: *"I keep tabs on what rattles him. If he makes an error, I will go back there again to see if there is a pattern."* Other comments included: *"I have a lot of variety, spins and speeds I can deploy, and I pay attention to what he doesn't like,"* and *"I find a weakness early, and I exploit it."*

A couple of respondents talked about standing in aggressively when returning serve and attacking on second serves. Relatedly, a few respondents talked about aggressively imposing their will. For example: *"I pull my opponent off the court with my serve and look to attack the net."* Another person commented: *"I look to attack them before they attack me."*

A couple of others talked about forcing their opponent to certain areas of the court (e.g., keeping them back, make them run and making them create their own angles).

Lastly, one person talked about using positive verbal and non-verbal gestures: *"I say to myself 'Come-on' and pump my fist."*

7. What are the most common reasons you have "choked" during matches?

Six respondents talked about how they started choking either because they were too consumed with the outcome and/or they let doubt crawl into their mind, so they lost confidence. One person commented: *"Usually I make some sort of judgment that I am supposed to win, and then I start to struggle when things are not going as planned."* Another said: *"I go into the match thinking the other team or opponent is weak and I am supposed to win easily, and when it doesn't happen, I start to press."*

A few respondents said it usually had to do with their nerves taking over, especially in big matches. One person commented: *"I get more nervous than normal when it is an important match, and I can also get tight and exhausted worrying about cramping – in which case I am pretty much done. When I am more nervous, cramps are more likely."*

A similar response had to do with getting *"super tight"* which caused him to get too tentative and to stop playing aggressively.

A couple of respondents said they were more likely to choke when having difficulty closing out the match: *"I start playing not to lose, instead of playing to win,"* and *"I have trouble playing up to my ability when I get close to finishing out a match."*

Lastly, a couple of interviewees said they were their own worst critic with negative thoughts and doubts. For example: *"I started thinking to myself, do I really have what it takes to win a tennis scholarship?"*

8. When playing big points, how do you change your approach (if applicable)? What strategies or tactics do you tend to use?

Several respondents said they try to play the same regardless of the score or match situation. *"I tell myself to play your game—that's what you should do. If my opponent gets nervous and tries to do something different or take a risk, that usually works to my advantage."* Another person commented: *"I tell myself to play the match, don't play the score."*

The second most popular response was to play the percentages, by not going for big shots, winners or line shots unless the opportunity presents itself. One person commented: *"I try to strike a balance between trying to be consistent to make my opponent earn the point and going for shots when I have an opening."*

Another theme was that you don't want to play it too safe or conservative. For example: *"When you get your ball, you have to hit it, and play to win."* And, *"I try to control the point from the outset."* Jeff Salzenstein pointed out that since his tendency was to hold back on big points, he would often tell himself to be more aggressive and *"swing for the fence"* or something to that affect.

A few respondents also talked about playing to their strengths or what has been working well in the match. For example: *"I try to get my first serve in and choose a serve that has worked well in the match."* Another person added: *"My game style is an aggressive one, so I am looking to apply pressure right away. I'm not going to play it safe just because it is 5 all in the 3rd set."*

Lastly, a few respondents talked about trying to be aggressive and take control of the point early. One commented: *"I like to plan out the first shots to set up the pattern I want to play so I can dictate the point. A serve plus one and return plus one."* Another person said: *"I used to hope the other player would miss on big points. I've learned I need to be super aggressive and raise my intensity."*

9. What do you try to do to learn from your losses?

The top theme that emerged was to analyze how/why you got outplayed and what you could have done better. One person noted: *"I'll play things over and over in my mind and think about what I could do differently the next time I play the same or similar opponent."*

A couple of respondents talked about going into more depth by watching video of the match with their coach and writing post-match notes which they would share and discuss with their coach.

Two interviewees (both junior players) talked about reflecting on the match to consider if they brought their best attitude and energy to the match.

Two other respondents talked about *"taking myself back to the same situations in practice* (i.e., same game or set score) *and then practice changing the behavior."*

Lastly, another important theme that came up was doing your best to move on or let it go quickly. Some have referred to this as the 24-hour rule. In other words, learn what you can from the loss, but avoid dwelling or obsessing about it so you'll have a positive outlook going into your next match.

10. What one piece of advice would you give to other players who struggle to play their best during match play?

There were a number of themes in response to this question. One popular one was to *"focus on what you can control."* The things you can control are having the right attitude and the mentality that you will fight/compete on every point. What you can't control, don't worry about.

Another popular response was to practice breathing on and off the court as a tool to help you relax. One person commented: *"Relax, breathe, and have fun."*

Another theme that came up was based on having good self-awareness: *"If your tendency is to make a lot of unforced errors, then play the percentages."* On the other hand, *"If your major issue is focus/concentration, then focus on your strategy and tactics."* Also, *"Play your strengths – play within yourself and your game."*

A few respondents talked about focusing on the big picture: *"Don't worry about today's results. Don't expect instant gratification. Focus more on what you want to accomplish in the long-term."*

Three people talked about the importance of developing good habits: *"It's all about discipline and hard work in practice."* Related comments included: *"Focusing on working hard and improving your game. The harder the training the better you will be."* A few others talked specifically about the importance of fitness: *"Get in better shape so you can compete harder and longer."*

A couple of respondents suggested using positive words/language. Jeff Salzenstein commented: *"Don't be a victim when you make errors. Instead, ask yourself what you can do differently."* Also, *"Use self-talk to give yourself directives on what to do."*

Two interviewees talked about having good awareness and then making necessary adjustments. One noted: *"Open your eyes and pay attention to what you are doing well and what your opponent is doing to hurt you. Then, make your adjustments."*

Former NCAA champion, Mark Merklein, said: *"I tell my players it is normal not to play your best in matches because you want to win so badly. Try to get to 70-75% of how you play in practice and be okay with that."*

Coach Steve Adamson commented: *"Don't give up. Keep working on the mental side of your game and you will eventually see better results."*

Lastly, Alexandra Osborne, WTA player, suggested: *"Play the ball, not the person. Focus on where the ball is coming from and where it will land. Who cares if your opponent in ranked higher, lower or is your friend. Tennis is all about angles and geometry."*

> 11. How do you stay self-motivated when times get tough (e.g., losses pile up, your budget is running low, you get injured, etc.)?

There was no highly repeated response to this question. A few interviewees talked about the importance of finding some balance. One commented: *"I don't play 7 days a week, so I can recharge mentally and physically."* Another person talked about the importance of cross-training, so it isn't all about tennis all the time.

A couple of people talked about how the recovery from injuries was tough, but it taught them to not over-train. A couple of respondents talked about spending more time doing mental training (i.e., visualization) and cutting down time on the court to help prevent more injuries.

A few respondents said it was relatively easy to stay optimistic because they are positive people. One person commented: *"My parents instilled in me a positive attitude. Everything happens for a reason and is a life lesson. I always believe that things will fall into place."* Another commented: *"I had back surgery my senior year in college resulting from pushing myself too hard. Staying motivated wasn't an issue though because tennis is my life."*

A couple of other interviewees said having a supportive team around them helped them to remain positive. One person said: *"Having supportive parents and a supportive coach makes a huge difference."* Another player commented: *"Me and my twin sister push and encourage each other."*

A few other respondents talked about trying to move on quickly. One noted: *"I don't dwell on things or hold grudges."* Another person said: *"I look forward to the next big match, and that keeps me motivated."*

One person commented that the losses motivated her to work harder and get in better shape. *"I learned how important it was to get in better shape off the court via cardio and weightlifting. If you are willing to work hard off the court, it makes you mentally and physically tougher on the court."*

Another person commented: *"I remind myself why I am playing. This helps me to start over and recharge after difficult losses. You have to love to compete and love to train."*

Lastly, one respondent said she learned to put the losses in perspective: *"I realized that my identity was not tied up with my tennis results and that I am more than just a tennis player. Having time away due to injuries also taught me to be a more well-rounded person which is important."*

Coach interview highlights

1. How do you go about gaining the trust of your players?

The top response was to show the players you care about them as human beings first. *"I take an interest in them as people and find out what they are passionate about outside of tennis."* One commented: *"When players see you care about them, you can be hard on them when necessary."*

A couple of coaches also talked about the importance of being a good listener and paying attention to what needs work (that is, their strokes, mental game or both). *"I find out what motivates them and what they are afraid of."*

A couple of other coaches talked about the importance of good, two-way communication. *"I look at it as a partnership and never talk down to my players."* Another commented: *"I want them to feel comfortable talking to me and not being afraid to tell me or ask me anything. Building a relationship helps in that regard."*

One coach talked about keeping things simple: *"I work on one thing at a time, so I don't overwhelm them."* Another coach commented: *"When I can show them how they can get better results they open up their receptors."*

2. What do you do on or off the court to help players develop a winning mentality and build up their self-confidence?

One theme that emerged was teaching players to be okay with making mistakes. *"I tell them it is okay to fail. "The only time you fail is when you don't try."* Another coach commented: *"If you want to have a great career, you have to learn to accept that it is okay to make mistakes. You also have to accept that there will be a lot of very highs and a lot of very lows along the way."*

Another theme was to teach players to be more self-reliant. One coach said: *"I teach them to be self-reliant and self-confident so that they eventually won't need me anymore."* Another commented: *"You can cheerlead and push, pull and scream, but ultimately it comes down to them. How hard are you willing to run and push yourself during that 10-minute drill?"*

One coach commented: *"I give them a lot of positive feedback to help build up their confidence. With some of my players who are overly confident, I focus more on their work ethic."* Lastly, one coach noted: *"I don't just want to develop the player, I want to develop the person and change their life."*

3. How do you coach a player who seems to be his/her own worst enemy and critic?

The top response was to get to know the player better and understand what motivates him/her. One coach commented: *"I try to analyze what is going on in their life. If they are stressed due to parent expectations, I will adjust based on their stress level."* Another respondent commented: *"I learn what makes them happy and more confident. I try to give them what they need. I believe if you are happier and more relaxed off the court, that will translate to playing better on the court."*

Another popular theme was working with the player to develop the best attitude. One coach said: *"I focus on having them develop the right attitude—they need to be playing for the right reasons, so they can get joy out of playing."* Another coach said, *"I teach them to eliminate excuses."*

A couple of coaches also talked about needing to address the negative self-talk. One said: *"I teach them to change their negative self-talk into positive self-talk. "Change your thoughts, change your life."* Another coach said: *"I have them practice using specific self-talk that will help them through difficult situations they will face during matches."*

4. What do you try to do to minimize the pressure placed on athletes to win, and keep things in perspective?

There was no dominant theme for this question. Highlights of their responses included:

"My slogan is you 'got to win the day' (not the match). Be in the present on that day. If you have a bad day, tomorrow will be better. Also, don't worry about what is coming up down the road."

"I coach them to give their best effort in practices, matches and in life, and not worry about the results. I teach them not to fear losing."

"Mix it up and keep things fun in practice. Playing other sports like ultimate Frisbee and soccer helps them to clear their head."

"Teach players to look forward to competing instead of fearing it. Competing is our reward for working hard in practice."

"I want the motivation to be intrinsic to the player. Not because they need to live up to someone else's expectations."

5. What additional recommendations do you have for coaching the mental side of tennis?

Again, there was no dominant theme. Here were some of their thoughts:

"I focus more on player development, and steer players away from needing instant gratification."

"I coach them less than more on match day. I try to keep things simple, so they don't overthink things."

"I try to have them focus on their game plan and shot selection, so their mind isn't cluttered with other thoughts."

"I have them practice their rituals over and over again, so they become automatic during match play."

"I teach them to give their best effort and have the right attitude, and not be worried about the match outcome."

"I have them work on visualizing how they want to play and also visualizing remaining calm and composed in difficult match situations."

"I teach them to be focused on the present, and to not get too high or too low based on anything that may happen in the match."

"I have my players put themselves mentally in tough spots and write out how they will handle it, so they feel fully prepared."

"I teach them to be self-reliant and encourage them to read books and watch videos of mentally tough players."

Lastly, one coach admitted that he should work more with players on mental training, however, he doesn't because the parents generally don't want that.

Parting shots: key takeaways, common themes, and surprises

#1 - Mental skills/mental toughness training doesn't get the attention it deserves

Coaches and players almost uniformly acknowledge that mental skills/mental toughness is the most critical element holding players back from reaching their potential. Nonetheless, less than half are actively doing anything about it. From the coaching perspective, most point out training players on mental toughness skills is not what the customer (that is, parents and players) want from coaches. This may be true, but what is also likely true is that many coaches don't know how to do it, are not properly trained, or are simply uncomfortable helping players deal effectively with the mental and emotional issues that get in the way of players reaching their full potential.

At the college level, most coaches have the luxury of referring players to sports psychologists (or other mental health professionals) to deal with mental and emotional issues. The progressive coaches, however, are minimally providing some form of mental training to help players maximize their performance. The more common mental skills areas addressed by coaches appear to be proper breathing techniques, using positive self-talk, and teaching players to focus on controlling the "controllables" (things within your control, like your attitude, effort, and focus), and not worrying about what you can't control (i.e., the weather, line calls, winning/losing the match, etc.).

I believe coaches would benefit by investing in training, so they are in a better position to help players develop their mental toughness skills and learn coping skills to get out of their own way. Additional training would also help coaches to identify when and why it is appropriate to refer players to mental health professionals, including sports psychologists.

#2 – Seeking instant gratification is your enemy

Many players, especially young players, make the mistake of expecting instant gratification or results. When they don't get the results they expect or want, this can lead to discouragement and possibly moving on from one coach to another. Players expecting instant gratification was cited as one of the biggest challenges coaches are facing.

As Dr. Larry Lauer, director of Player Development for USTA noted: *"You have to have faith that the process will get you to where you want to be."* Further: *"Players should always be striving to win, but more importantly, they need a willingness to commit to a process that doesn't bear fruit for quite a while."* A good coach (minimally, a coach that you fully trust) will get you to buy into a process or long-term plan for development.

As coach Brett Kurtz advises, players should delay evaluations and judgments, and instead, keep working to get better day by day. Most of your focus should ideally be on the process of getting better, and not on results. It may be helpful, however, to focus on the outcome or results when you are pushing yourself to work harder in practice (when you are tired and sore) and off the court (on the track and/or in the gym) to motivate you to do everything in your power to prepare yourself to compete to the best of your ability. Your goal each day should be to feel proud of the way you competed when you walk off the court – win or lose. With that type of attitude, it will take the edge and the pressure off trying to win now.

Smart coaches will help players to focus less on wins/losses and more on the improvement process and developmental needs. Losing the focus on results is key to player growth, satisfaction, stress management, and avoiding burnout. Parents and coaches should help to reinforce player effort, commitment, discipline, and positive attitude instead of results.

#3 – Training your mind to focus on the present will lead to improved results and more fun competing

During competition, if your mind is focused on the past or the future, it will invariably have a negative impact on your performance. Focusing on the past (such as, the point or game you just lost) or the future (that is, winning or losing the match) generally brings your mind to a negative or unproductive place. Basically, anything that doesn't allow you to be fully present and immersed in what you are doing, will have a detrimental effect on your performance.

A future orientation results in a lot of "what ifs" that lead to more worry, anxiousness, nervousness, stress and pressure. The what ifs, are thoughts like: What if I miss this shot? What if I get broken? What if I lose this match? Or, what if I let my teammates or parents down?

A past orientation typically means you are experiencing anger, frustration, regret, or possibly even depression over something that has happened like missed opportunities, previous losses, or a bad calls by your opponent. So, when you find yourself feeling angry or frustrated, this can be your trigger or reminder that you don't have a present orientation.

While it is impossible to prevent our brains from shifting to thinking about the past or future, what we can do is learn to recognize and acknowledge these thoughts and feelings when they occur, and then quickly make a choice to pivot back to what is going on in the present (that is, the next point). Remember, the present moment is the only place you can be at your best and potentially experience flow or be in the zone.

To promote a present orientation or mindset, Coach Brett Kurtz repeatedly tells his players—*"It doesn't matter what the score is – it's always zero-zero."* He also firmly believes that the ability to let go of results is critical to their success and happiness.

As covered in this book, practicing mindful meditation is a great way to improve your ability to be accepting of the situation you are in, and maintain a positive and present orientation when experiencing adversity. Also, being aware of your thought patterns during matches can serve as a reminder to stay present and refocus back to the task at hand.

#4 – Being able to refocus quickly is critical to your success

Since there is only 30 seconds between points, one key to being mentally tough is having the ability to refocus quickly. This is part of the reason why having a consistent ritual between points can be very beneficial.

Don't be disappointed with yourself when your mind wanders throughout your match. It is perfectly normal to be distracted by your thoughts and what is going on around you on the court. The goal should be to refocus back to the next point, so you can compete to the best of your ability.

Thirty (30) seconds between points is not a lot of time, however, with practice you can gather your thoughts, refocus (with or without a ritual) and determine what you want to do tactically in the next point.

#5 - Effective breathing is an underrated asset

One important thing you can control, and learn to do better with practice, is how you breathe between points and between games. Learning to inhale and exhale effectively is a very powerful way to allow your mind to quiet, and to bring your heart rate down when under pressure. The key is being able to consistently repeat your breathing routine when under duress.

Although committing to mindful meditation on a daily basis is the recommended way to learn to consistently breathe effectively, you can also work on your breathing out on the courts or on the track. One way to do so is to run sprints, and then practice breathing in deeply and exhaling slowly after each sprint. By doing so, you can learn to recognize what it feels like to have your heart rate elevated, and how you can use your breath to bring your heart rate down and feel more relaxed. By teaching yourself to recover more quickly, it will help you think more clearly and make better decisions in your matches.

#6 - Players benefit from taking ownership for their tennis results and developing their game

One of the themes repeated often by players and coaches was the importance of taking ownership for everything associated with your performance. This is an important step in a tennis player's maturation process.

In the absence of taking ownership or being self-driven, players will more likely be lacking in motivation, and will experience less joy in the day-to-day process of working on their game.

According to former ATP pros, Mark Merklein and Jeff Salzenstein, players should be asking a lot of questions, and always be looking for ways to get better. Self-reliant players are more engaged and are also better at overcoming obstacles. My belief is that self-reliant players are also more likely to take the initiative to work hard on their fitness, conditioning, and technical skills when no one else is watching (such as during COVID-19). That's the sort of personal commitment and dedication required to maximize your potential.

Today's young prodigies (including young pros) often lack independent skill sets according to several of the coaches I interviewed. Coaches also run the risk of increasing player dependency on others when they "overcoach," by providing ongoing feedback after almost every point in practice. Providing excessive feedback can make players overly reliant on the coach. Players who are overly reliant on coaching feedback will start to lose the ability to think for themselves and will be less likely to be able to problem-solve on their own. As we covered earlier in this book, one of the keys to winning more matches is being able to figure out what is working, and not working, so you can problem-solve on the fly during matches.

Another key to developing self-reliance in players is for coaches to ask a lot of questions, instead of relying primarily or solely on providing feedback. For example, asking questions like: "What could you have done differently on that point?" helps to build player self-reliance and also serves to increase their tennis IQ.

#7 - Elite tennis players struggle with issues of self-confidence, self-doubt, nerves and anxiousness just like the rest of us do.

The interviews I conducted for this book made it abundantly clear that ATP pros and other highly successful players deal with self-belief and confidence issues, similar to competitive players at all levels. I had erroneously assumed that once players reach a certain status, they would be somewhat immune to such issues. In retrospect, this shouldn't be shocking to learn, as they are only human, like the rest of us. As John Isner commented: *"It's the same for everyone. Everyone battles the same demons out there. Everyone's had their tough losses."* Multi-grand slam winner, Maria Sharapova, had similar sentiments: *"Even when you are a champion and you come off the court losing, you ask yourself am I good enough? You are always searching to find who you are and where you'll go."*

Former ATP pros, Diego Ayala, and Mark Merklein, also talked about how they struggled with confidence, especially early in their career. They revealed that self-belief issues never really go away completely. It is comforting in a way to learn that players with great resumes like Mark Merklein, former NCAA champion and pro, are just like the rest of us. In other words, if they can achieve greatness in spite of these mental demons and challenges, there is hope for the rest of us.

Perhaps all-time great champions like Djokovic and Serena Williams don't suffer as much or as often from confidence or self-belief issues as the rest, but even all-time greats like Federer have had their moments. The Jeff Salzenstein's story I shared about his match with Michael Chang highlights the self-belief differences that may separate the truly elite pros from the rest. In some of the biggest matches of his life, Jeff would wonder: *"Who is going to show up today, Little Jeff or Big Jeff?"*

Dr. Jim Taylor, Sports Psychologist, speaking on a podcast with Dr. Cindra Kamphoff entitled: "Developing the Mind of a Champion" commented: *"The biggest struggles with confidence and self-esteem issues for many players often results from the "deeper" stuff like overinvestment in their sport. As a result, their self-esteem is too connected to their results."*

#8 - Perfectionism is a common problem for high achieving tennis players

Based on my interviews and research, perfectionism is a fairly common issue for top players. Coach Peter Smith commented how he has coached many players with perfectionist tendencies in his long career as the highly successful USC Men's tennis coach.

On the positive side, perfectionism can have the benefit of pushing players to work extra hard to achieve their goals. On the downside, however, it can interfere with players achieving their highest level, because they are unwilling to take the risks needed to get there. Perfectionism is striving for a goal they can never achieve. When they fail to achieve perfection, players beat themselves up. It is like a personal attack on their value as a person.

Although I don't believe I personally have perfectionist tendencies, I did struggle with needing to feel completely in control of what my body was doing, especially in tournament play. Essentially, I was trying too hard instead of relaxing, letting go and fully trusting that my training and hard work had prepared me to do my best. As a result, I tended to overthink things, and it made me reluctant to take sufficient risks during matches. After my college playing days were over, I learned to relax and trust myself and let my body or muscle memory take over. I essentially got out of my own way and didn't worry about my stroke mechanics or other distracting thoughts and trusted that my training had prepared me to do well. This mindset also made it much more enjoyable to compete—an added bonus.

Dr. Jim Thompson, sports psychologist, believes the antidote for perfectionism is to strive for excellence instead, because excellence allows for mistakes. It is essential to make mistakes—it means you are taking risks and moving out of your comfort zone. Without taking calculated risks, you are not truly giving everything that you've got.

Based on my research, I believe that some perfectionists may also be suffering from the *"Imposter Syndrome"*—the idea that you've only succeeded due to luck, and not because of your talent and qualifications. The imposter syndrome was first identified by psychologists, Pauline Rose Clance and Suzanne Imes (source: "Yes, Imposter Syndrome is Real. Here's How to Deal with It", by Abigail Abrams, Time.com, June 20, 2018).

Perfectionists may have *"imposter"* feelings because they set extremely high expectations for themselves, and even if they meet over 90% of their goals, they're going to feel like failures. Any small mistake will make them question their own competence. As this article points out, most people experience moments of doubt, which is normal. The important thing is not to let that doubt control your actions. With this insight, *"They can still have imposter moments, but don't have to have an imposter life."*

#9 - Play to win, not to avoid losing!

Perhaps the most important and recurring takeaway from my interviews and research is that many players have had to overcome a fear of failure. It may be helpful to first consider how you define failure. If your definition of failure is not winning the tournament, then everyone fails except the tournament winners. A better thought process in my mind is that you have not failed, unless you have failed to learn. Or, another way to look at it is that you need to be willing to endure a whole lot of defeats if you will eventually become a champion or reach your potential.

In order to reach your potential, I would argue you need to learn to be okay with losing, and not worrying about failure. As Dr. Cindra Kamphoff, sports psychologist, noted on her "High Performance Mindset" podcast: *"Failure leads you to the path that you are supposed to be on."*

Viewing failure or losing as an opportunity to learn is a paradigm shift for many, so I don't see it as a mindset one can achieve by flipping a switch. Also, since we live in an outcome or results-oriented society, in a sense you have to go against the grain when deciding or committing to not worrying about "failure" or losing.

Rafael Nadal has a productive mindset on losing that all of us could benefit from emulating. Fear of failure or losing doesn't make him worry or become more anxious. Instead, fear of losing pushes him to improve and make adjustments, and also work harder in practice.

Although he'll do anything in his power to avoid losing, he understands and accepts that losing some matches is inevitable when you are going up against great players like Federer and Djokovic.

Dr. Jim Taylor believes that it is very common for tennis players and other athletes to be driven by fear of failure, instead of trying to achieve success. *"The goal is to learn to deal with failure and recognize that it won't kill you. You will learn something and will be okay regardless of your tennis results."* If tennis players, and other athletes, can buy into this logic, they free themselves from that "50-pound weight vest" and it is liberating. Essentially, the advice is to free yourself from such concerns and just do what you trained to do, and not let other things get in your way like worrying about results, rankings and living up to others' expectations.

In the final analysis, playing to win comes down to making a commitment – to play the way you want to play and not be afraid of the results. **The goal is to be fully present, compete your heart out and play with no regrets. That is the optimal way you give yourself the best chance to realize your full potential.**

(This page intentionally left blank.)

About the authors

David Zobler

My name is David Zobler. I have played competitive tennis for over 40 years. I was captain of my high school and college tennis teams, have experience as a high school tennis coach and teaching pro, and have had success playing in United States Tennis Association tournaments after college. I also completed a master's degree in psychology at Columbia University.

This book is for tennis players who have put in the hours of on-court practice, who have worked on their off-court conditioning, who have changed their diets, who have changed their racquets, swapped out their strings, and have gone through numerous tennis shoes searching for the magic recipe to give him or her the winning edge.

I have always been intrigued by the psychological aspects of tennis. Why do we lose tennis matches that we should or could win? What creates the barriers to success and how can we overcome them?

To delve deeper into this topic, I have reached out to expert coaches, players, and sports psychologists for their invaluable insights. I hope you find their answers as enlightening and game changing as I have.

David

Tom Aguilar

My name is Tom Aguilar. I grew up and lived my entire life in sunny Southern California. I fell in love with the game of tennis the first time I saw Wimbledon broadcast on a black-and-white television screen. I did not know what this game was, but I wanted to play it. I first picked up a used racquet and hit balls on our wooden garage door constantly. Little circles of tennis ball imprints peppered our track home garage door permanently. My first foray into repetition and mental training. I was 12 years old and we had just moved to a new neighborhood where I didn't know anyone. I tried out for the tennis team at the new school and somehow made the team.

My father, Arnold, picked up tennis instructional books and learned the game to teach it to me. My dad never played sports growing up. As a child, his mom carried him with a wrap that cut into his chest muscle, damaging it. He was always self-conscious about the way his body looked and never wanted to remove his shirt for organized sports. Every day when dad got home from work, we would jump in his car and take a 5-gallon white bucket of used balls and he would feed me balls and instruct me on the things he learned in the tennis books and in tennis magazines.

I began to get better with constant practice. I played in high school and won the Hacienda League championship my senior year at Ontario High School in Southern California. I played at Mount San Antonio College, known as Mount SAC, for one season on the traveling team. I stopped playing and I got a job and eventually married and had two wonderful kids, Kyle and Elizabeth. After about 10 years, friends asked if I played and we started playing on the weekends. The love of tennis never died; it had just been dormant.

I coached my son in a local youth tennis league for boys and girls from 8 to 18 years old for several years. After my divorce, I moved close to the beach, eliminated my commute, and started playing again in earnest. I played as often as I could. My efforts eventually culminated when I won the Manhattan Beach Open 4.0 singles title in 2019. To this day, I still play in a USTA league on the Palos Verdes Tennis Team. In 2019, the team I played on a 9.0 men's doubles team that went to nationals in Surprise, Arizona, where we took 5th place overall. Currently, I play weekly with a great group of players. Today, my partner, Joanna, and I enjoy healthy eating, cross-training (biking, yoga, weightlifting), and international travel.

The mental side of the game has always fascinated me. As my game developed and became more well-rounded, an opponent with equal skills, but a tougher mental game would always defeat me. I learned that, like any muscle, if you exercise it, you can develop it and make it stronger.

I hope the compiled lessons can help jumpstart you in your mental toughness journey.

Tom

(This page intentionally left blank.)

Index

24-hour rule, 178
Alexandra Osborne, 48, 64, 141, 153, 180
Alexis Castorri, 133
Allen Fox, 4, 21, 40, 87, 88, 89
Allon Khakshouri, 22, 113, 119
Amber McGinnis, 25, 37, 49, 50, 51, 52, 54, 80, 122, 141
Andre Agassi, 9, 22, 32, 35, 37, 75, 107, 141
Andy Murray, 35, 133, 134
Andy Roddick, 12
Anja Tomljanovic, 83
Anne Grady, 28, 84
Arnold Aguilar, iv
Awareness of Breath, 107
bare awareness, 108
Ben Simmons, 129
big points, 34, 35, 36, 37, 84, 101, 145, 147, 152, 155, 175, 177, 178
Bill Cole, 13
Billie Jean King, 166
Bjorn Borg, xv, 89
Brad Gilbert, 16, 30
breathing, 8, 11, 14, 28, 40, 107, 108, 112, 113, 115, 117, 118, 122, 131, 153, 154, 169, 170, 171, 173, 179, 187, 191
Brett Kurtz, 41, 70, 75, 116, 121, 132, 141, 165, 188, 190
British Journal of Sports Medicine, 130
Bruce Kurtz, 141, 152
Calm, 113, 115
cardio, 181
Carlos Alcaraz, 17, 37
Carol Dweck, 73
character traits, 69
choking, 12, 13, 14, 176
Chris Evert, 89, 140
Cindra Kamphoff, 28, 127, 194, 196
coaching feedback, 34, 192
Coco Gauff, 27
confidence, xv, xvi, xvii, 1, 3, 4, 5, 6, 7, 16, 21, 23, 25, 28, 33, 37, 45, 46, 76, 84, 100, 123, 124, 126, 127, 133, 145, 155, 157, 164, 175, 176, 183, 184, 193, 194
constructing points, 45
COVID-19, 102, 118, 192
Craig O'Shannessy, 23
Craig Sigl, 99
Daniel Dauber, 141

Darren Cahill, 136
Darrin Donnelly, 5, 22
David Zobler, ii, xv, 199
Dean Smith, 164
Deena Kastor, 133
Denis Shapovalov, 87
Diego Ayala, 10, 55, 130, 139, 150, 162, 193
Dominic Thiem, 38
Duncan Simpson, 98, 122, 127
Ebony Panoho, 64, 141
emotions, xi, 25, 28, 36, 40, 71, 87, 88, 89, 92, 93, 97, 103, 108, 116, 117, 120, 126, 127
Eugenie Bouchard, 55, 139
excuses, 15, 20, 21, 22, 33, 71, 89, 95, 153, 185
Felix Auger-Aliassime, 42
flow, 110, 111, 112, 136, 190
focus, xv, 8, 11, 13, 16, 17, 18, 19, 20, 21, 23, 31, 33, 34, 35, 36, 41, 71, 77, 78, 80, 85, 92, 95, 96, 97, 98, 99, 100, 101, 102, 103, 105, 109, 113, 116, 117, 118, 121, 122, 124, 131, 133, 135, 149, 151, 152, 155, 156, 169, 170, 171, 173, 175, 179, 184, 186, 187, 188, 189
George Bezecny, 56, 57, 99, 140, 151, 170
George Mumford, 4, 33, 107
Goran Ivanisevic, 20, 160
Gretchen Rush, 143
Harold Solomon, 101
Headspace, 113, 115
Imposter Syndrome, 195
instant gratification nation, 76
Instant Timer, 113, 115
Jack Bauerle, 72, 73, 99, 140, 163
Jack Nicholas, 105
Jake Li, 60, 61, 62, 63
James Blake, 139
James Clear, 77, 99, 121
Jeff Salzenstein, 13, 41, 46, 85, 104, 121, 123, 137, 146, 160, 177, 179, 192, 194
Jeff Thomsen, 142, 154, 166
Jelena Jankovic, 139
Jim Afremow, 18, 73, 83, 104, 116
Jim Courier, 10, 13, 101
Jim Dinkmeyer, 75
Jim Golby, 91
Jim Loehr, 27, 39, 41, 77, 103, 121

Jim Taylor, 27, 194, 197
Jim Thompson, 103, 195
Jimmy Connors, xv, 3, 89, 101
John Isner, 193
John McEnroe, xv, 1, 24, 35, 37, 133, 134
John O'Sullivan, 69, 72
John Wooden, 24, 25, 164
Jonathan Fromkin, 49, 53, 70, 118
Justin Gimelstob, 44, 138
Justine Henin, 91
Kerry Reid, 143
Kevin Anderson, 101, 133, 135
Kevin Love, 129
Larry Lauer, 188
Larry Willens, 85, 118, 143, 155, 167
Laurie Johnson, 91
Layne Beachley, 119
Lennie Waite, 125
Lindsay Graff, 141
losing, xii, xvii, 2, 3, 6, 7, 10, 11, 14, 15, 17, 21, 22, 25, 29, 76, 79, 88, 89, 101, 104, 109, 111, 134, 136, 145, 146, 151, 159, 168, 172, 173, 174, 175, 185, 187, 189, 193, 196

Ludwik and Phyllis Zobler, iv
Mack Brown, 159
Maria Sakkari, 9
Maria Sharapova, 193
Mark Merklein, 125, 131, 138, 141, 148, 161, 180, 192, 193
Marty Fish, 129
Matteo Berrettini, 27
meditation, 107, 108, 112, 113, 115, 159, 190, 191
mental health, 129, 130, 187, 188
mental toughness, xviii, 27, 39, 71, 72, 77, 79, 91, 93, 97, 98, 99, 100, 101, 102, 103, 120, 131, 133, 148, 151, 187, 188, 201
Michael Chang, 24, 123, 194
Michael Jordan, 88, 105
Michael Sheard, 91
Michelle and Samara Eisenberg, 58
Michelle Cleere, 8, 118
Michelle Eisenberg, 59, 80, 122
Mihaly Csikszentmihalyi, 111
Mindfulness, 107, 108
Morgan Shepherd, 71

Naomi Osaka, 129
Noelle Aguilar, iv
Novak Djokovic, 3, 5, 8, 13, 29, 35, 112
optimal performance, 96
Patrick Cohn, 93, 104
Patrick Mouratoglou, 130
Paul Annacone, 9, 10, 16
Paul Goldstein, 4, 91, 131
Pauline Rose Clance, 195
Perfectionism, 194
performance development goals, 78, 165
Pete Sampras, xv, 10, 13, 32, 76, 141
Peter Scales, 71
Peter Smith, xi, xii, 9, 12, 18, 105, 110, 137, 145, 157, 194
Petra Kvitova, 27
Rafael Nadal, 5, 6, 9, 14, 19, 20, 69, 121, 196
Rick Macci, 39, 69
rituals, xviii, 31, 40, 41, 77, 78, 102, 117, 118, 120, 121, 146, 153, 165, 171, 173, 186
Rob Rotella, 73
Robby Ginepri, 139
Robin White, 143
Rod Laver, 17, 143
Roger Federer, 1, 5, 10, 13, 14, 17, 89, 139, 141, 148
Sam Querrey, 137
Samara Eisenberg, 58, 59
Self-Talk, 83
Serena Williams, 19, 24, 69, 123, 130, 148, 193
Simona Halep, 133, 136
sports psychologists, 130, 187, 188, 199
Steffi Graf, 17
Stephanie Taylor, 52, 141
Steve Adamson, 142, 155, 167, 180
Steve Johnson, xi, xiii, 137
Superman, 148
Suzanne Imes, 195
The Four Cs, 105
Todd Widom, 44
Tom Aguilar, ii, 200
Tomas Muster, 101
Toni Nadal, 20, 69, 71
Tony Robbins, 33
Venus Williams, 3
Vic Braden, 42
video feedback, 34
Viktor Frankl, 109
Vince Spadea, 141
visualization, 115, 116, 117, 118, 119, 120, 135, 156, 159, 169, 181

W. Timothy Gallwey, 13, 109
weightlifting, 181

why you lose, 1
Winston Churchill, 109
Zoe Scandalis, 143

Made in the USA
Columbia, SC
01 May 2024